The
Exodus Pattern
in the Bible

ALL SOULS STUDIES

II

The
Exodus Pattern
in the Bible

ALL SOULS STUDIES

*

*A series of monographs by past and present
Fellows of All Souls College, Oxford*

THE
EXODUS PATTERN
IN THE BIBLE

by

DAVID DAUBE, F.B.A.

Fellow of All Souls College, Oxford
Regius Professor of Civil Law in the
University of Oxford
D.C.L., Ph.D., Dr. Jur., Hon. LL.D.

WIPF & STOCK · Eugene, Oregon

Wipf and Stock Publishers
199 W 8th Ave, Suite 3
Eugene, OR 97401

The Exodus Pattern in the Bible
By Daube, David
Copyright © 1963 by Daube, David All rights reserved.
Softcover ISBN-13: 978-1-7252-7499-0
Publication date 3/26/2020
Previously published by Faber, 1963

To
REUVEN
and
SHOSHANNA

Contents

I

The Pattern

To this day the narrative of the exodus inspires those who recount the disasters and salvations of Israel, ancient or modern, secular or spiritual. 'Ils sont partis', sings Edith Piaf, 'courir la mer. Délivrez-nous, nos frères! Et leurs frères les ont tirés vers la lumière.' As is well known, this habit of looking on the exodus as a prototype, as a mould in which other stories of rescue from ruin may be cast, goes back to the Bible itself. The account of Joshua's crossing of the Jordan is full of elements designed to recall the crossing of the red sea under Moses.[1] In the second century B.C. Ben-Sira prays for a repetition of 'signs and wonders' — he means final redemption, thought of in terms of the exodus.[2] Exactly that has come to pass, according to Acts,[3] through Jesus — a second Moses, leading forth his people a second time.

At one time I planned to write on Patterns of Deliverance in the Bible, believing that there must be several of about equal eminence. I soon discovered that there was none remotely comparable to the exodus. That epic stands out in imposing its presuppositions and categories on others. Of course, different patterns do exist, but they are very minor in comparison. At first sight one would think that such a general one as that dominant in the Book of Judges must be independent: calamity befalls the children of Israel when

[1] Cp. e.g. Jo 4.6f., 21f., with Ex 12.26f., D, 13.14, D, Dt 6.20f. In assigning Pentateuchic texts to sources, we base on Skinner, *Genesis*, 2nd ed., 1930; Beer, *Exodus*, 1939; and Gray, *Numbers*, 1912. Refinements such as the distinction between J[1] and J[2] will be suppressed.

[2] Si 36.6; see Rengstorf, s.v. *semeion*, *Theologisches Wörterbuch zum Neuen Testament*, ed. Friedrich, 7, 1961, 219f.

[3] 2.19, 22; Rengstorf, 239f.

they turn from God, but he relents when they 'cry' to him.[1] From the phraseology alone, however, it is obvious that even here the exodus is serving as model: God had been moved by the 'cry' of those oppressed in Egypt.[2] On the other hand, the Book of Judith suggests that some tales from Judges did play a part with later bards. Judges has three female saviours, the woman who dropped a millstone on Abimelech's head, Jael and Deborah.[3] The two former were killers, and the parallel between Judith and Jael, close in several respects, is stressed in the Book of Judith.[4] Quite possibly, the author had also in mind the story of Ehud,[5] who brought the king of Moab a present and asked for a private audience; stabbed him; escaped before the murder was detected; and called on his fellow-countrymen to fight and exploit the panic caused by the king's death. But again, the ultimate release of the Israelites from Egypt occurs as a result of the terror experienced by the Egyptians on discovering that their firstborn are slain. At any rate it is a question of a relatively unimportant motif.

It is not as if the Bible were lacking in potential models of a major character. We need only think of the narratives of the flood, of Abraham, of Joseph, of Samson and of David. Yet though ideas and features are freely borrowed from these and others — as when Jesus is assimilated to David[6] or Mary to Ruth[7] — this is done only on special occasions and for special purposes, and even then the borrowing is confined to details. It is never, as in the case of the exodus, the story as a whole into the framework of which new events are forced. No doubt the principal reason for the fascination exercised by the exodus is that here was depicted — in vivid colours, with ups and downs, in detail open to variable interpretation, and paying equal attention to material and sacred needs and

---

[1] Judg 3.9, 15, 4.3, 6.6f., 10.10, 12, 14; see Moore, *Judges*, 1895, 62f.

[2] See below, p. 27.

[3] Judg 9.53, 4.21, 4.4ff. Cp. the wise woman in 2 Sm 20.16ff.

[4] Judg 4.9 echoed in Ju 9.10, 13.15, 14.18, 16.6ff., and Judg 5.24 in Ju 13.18.

[5] Judg 3.15ff.

[6] A possible example Lk 2.8; see Rengstorf, *Das Evangelium nach Lukas*, 9th ed., 1962, 41.

[7] Lk 1.35, 38; see Daube, *The New Testament and Rabbinic Judaism*, 1956, 27ff. The Nunc dimittis in 2.29 uses the same method as 1.35 to suggest an analogy — this time between Simeon and Abraham; see Daube, Novum Testamentum 5, 1962, 102.

fulfilments — the first great deliverance, indeed, the birth, of the nation.

But there is a consideration to be added, less important but not negligible. The authors of the story of the exodus at vital points made use of concepts familiar to them from the social laws and customs of their time. According to these, a Hebrew slave was to be treated with some consideration; given certain conditions, his nearest relative had the right and duty to recover him for his original family, or he himself might buy back his freedom; in any case he was to be released at the end of a definite period; and even a captive in foreign hands, we shall see, might hope to be ransomed or otherwise freed by a friend at home sufficiently powerful and loyal. Rules similar in spirit applied to family property which an impoverished owner had been forced to dispose of: it was not to be lost to him or the family for ever. Furthermore, the crime of murder was closely allied, under that social order, to the illicit subjugation of a person. It was up to the nearest relative of the victim to exact retribution and, thereby, to recover the blood shed. The authors of the exodus story represented Pharaoh as flouting established social regulations, and God as making him comply with them, *malgré lui*, or suffer the sanctions of his breaches. They construed the exodus as an enforcement of legal claims. As one example of many we may quote God's demand to Pharaoh:[1] 'Israel is my son. . . . Let my son go.'

The consequence was to lift the exodus out of the sphere of the accidental, the arbitrary, the mythological and, instead, to link it to norms of — in the eyes of the authors and their successors — eternal validity. It is from that moment that Biblical salvation acquired that connection with ethics and justice, social and international, which marks it off throughout the centuries from otherwise comparable Oriental and Hellenistic notions. God was seen as intervening, not like a despot, but in the faithful exercise of a recognized privilege — which would, in turn, impose lasting obligations on those on whose behalf he intervened; we shall come back to this aspect. What we are at the moment concerned with is the confidence and stability which resulted from this anchoring in firm legal relations. As God had vindicated those relations in the

[1] Ex 4.22f., J.

exodus, one could be certain that he would vindicate them again, and again, unto the last. The kind of salvation portrayed in the exodus was not, by its nature, an isolated occurrence, giving rise to nebulous hopes for similar good luck in the future: it had its root in, and set the seal on, a permanent institution — hence it was something on which absolute reliance might be placed. Surely, this particular quality must have greatly contributed to the coming into existence and popularity of the pattern. By being fashioned on the exodus, later deliverances became manifestations of this eternal, certainty-giving relationship between God and his people. It will emerge as we go on that, conceivably, even events prior to the exodus were made to approximate the latter, so as to gain still earlier proof of this role of God.

Though a good deal has been written on exodus typology,[1] the subject is far from exhausted. For instance, little has been done on how its role in national redemption is related to its role in re-demption of the individual. A few remarks will be found scattered in the following pages.[2] The aim of the present essay, however, is a very limited one; namely, to call attention to the social and legal affiliations of the pattern generally neglected, and to say something about their antecedents and effects. Even so, completeness will not be attempted. I have dealt with several aspects elsewhere and do not propose to repeat every single observation.[3]

There are, moreover, two interesting questions which will be left undiscussed because their ramifications are too wide; it is hoped that others, more competent, will take them up. First, it would be legitimate to ask whether there was once an exodus story not yet following the lines indicated. This is not improbable, though it would have to antedate any of the sources represented in the Pentateuch, J, E, P and D. As will be shewn, all four offer illustrations of that construction of the exodus, as the freeing of a slave in accordance with social legislation or practice. Secondly, if

[1] A recent study: Zimmerli, 'Le Nouvel "Exode" Dans Le Message Des Deux Grands Prophètes De L'Exil', in *La branche d'amandier*, 1960, 216ff.

[2] See pp. 21, 27, 70, 82.

[3] See *Studies in Biblical Law*, 1947, 39ff.; Archiv Orientálni 17, 1949, 88ff.; *The New Testament and Rabbinic Judaism*, 1956, 5ff., 158ff., 268ff.; 'Rechtsgedanken in den Erzählungen des Pentateuchs', in *Von Ugarit nach Qumran*, 1958, 35ff.; New Testament Studies 5, 1959, 174ff.

the view here taken of what the authors of the exodus narrative had in mind is correct, that must have a decisive bearing on their cultural and political background; on their contacts with and interest in usages such as survive in Biblical codes early and late, the Book of the Covenant, the Priestly Code, Deuteronomy; on their and their public's attitude to might and right, wealth and poverty, freedom and slavery, family, society and inter-state commerce; and indeed on the communal object of their narrative — in brief, on its setting in life, its *Sitz im Leben*. The promulgation of such a unique concept of deliverance, in (as will become clear) a highly elaborate form, does not take place in a vacuum. In a less degree, the same goes for those who adopted the pattern, describing other happenings in the same terms. I suspect that the current theories as to the setting of the exodus and narratives drawing on it will need to be radically revised.

II

Problems of Method

The exodus was construed as an application, on a higher plane, of social usages familiar to the authors of the story from their daily world. Once the story in this form had gained currency, however, it in its turn had an enormous impact on social affairs. Once it was believed that the nation owed nothing less than its existence to those laws and customs — enforced by God — the significance of this area of life was immeasurably enhanced. Among the deeper historical causes of the extraordinary role played by social ethics in Judaism for some three thousand years, the narrative of the exodus with its orientation towards justice deserves a foremost place. Certainly the Pentateuch reinforces much social legislation with references to that deliverance. For instance, the Deuteronomic version of the commandment of Sabbatical rest for all the household contains the addition,[1] 'in order that thy manservant and thy maidservant may rest like thee, and remember that thou wast a servant in Egypt and that the Lord thy God brought thee out.' Indeed, we find reinforced in this way, or even represented as having their *raison d'être* in the exodus, some of those very statutes which, or precursors of which, had been in the minds of the authors of the narrative. Thus a Hebrew slave, we are told, is to go out free in the jubilee, 'for they are my slaves which I brought out of Egypt.'[2]

We may, then, distinguish three stages: there is the ancient social practice, there is the exodus depicting God as acting in conformity with that practice, and there is social practice advancing under the stimulus of the story. This development is not unusual.

[1] Dt 5.14f.   [2] Lv 25.42.

Problems of Method

The institution of kingship may be compared, first growing up on earth; then God's rule is construed by analogy; and finally his kingship confers increased dignity and new meanings on the original institution. In the wide field of *imitatio Dei* (or *herois*) it has long been seen that there is a constant give and take of this sort. The start is from an admired human quality, mercy, magnanimity; then God is clothed with it; and now the divine attribute becomes a high ideal and a fresh source of progress in human intercourse.[1]

At this point it may be useful to deal with some problems of method. How do we know about social usages on which, it is here postulated, the exodus narrators drew? Largely — though not exclusively — from sources later than the narrative. For example, it is the Priestly Code[2] which declares that a Hebrew slave who sold himself to an alien (a resident alien) may be bought back by a relative. Does this not rule out the possibility of the practice having influenced the story? It does not. A law may considerably antedate the source in which it is transmitted. To be sure, we must make allowance for likely variation in detail; and often custom, not couched in precise terms, rather than a statute may have to be reckoned with at the earlier stage. But this does not affect the main point. Indeed, the earlier allusion in the story may be very illuminating as to the growth of the law, we may learn from it what the practice was like before being given its final shape. The scene in the Odyssey[3] where Hephaestus catches his wife with Ares, and Poseidon goes bail for the latter, enables us, by a judicious combination with post-Homeric material, to trace back many of the later rules concerning adultery, the position of a surety and so on.[4] Judicious the combination must be; naturally it is a delicate operation to decide whether and to what extent an institution ordained at a given time may be seen reflected, or adumbrated, in previous statements. In the next chapter we shall set out some rough-and-ready criteria to go by.

There are subtler difficulties. We shall find that both J and E (and maybe P as well), in recounting the exodus, make God apply a

---

[1] See Abrahams, *Studies in Pharisaism and the Gospels*, Second Series, 1924, 138ff.
[2] Lv 25.47ff. [3] 8.306ff.
[4] See Partsch, *Griechisches Bürgschaftsrecht*, 1st pt., 1909, 9ff.

principle met in — the later — D, namely, that a slave should be
released with gifts; and one passage, probably J though attribution
to E is defensible, has almost the exact phrasing of D.[1] So far no
fundamental objection could be raised: we have just pointed out
that there is nothing strange in a law transmitted by a relatively
late source being known to and made use of by story-tellers of an
earlier age. But E contains a code, the Book of the Covenant,
which, like D, deals with release of slaves; yet it makes no mention
of gifts.[2] In these circumstances, is it still tenable that, in its narrative portion, about the exodus, E should be acquainted with such
gifts? It is still tenable. For one thing, the opposite view proceeds
from too rigid a notion — and one happily out of date — of what is
meant by a source like E (or J or P). E stands for 'the Elohist'. But
we must not be misled by this label into thinking of a single person
who spontaneously invented and wrote down all that is found in the
source, tales, laws, moral injunctions, prophecies. It is not even a
single compiler. E designates a stratum of tradition which, while
having certain unifying characteristics, is highly composite as
regards ultimate provenance and bears the marks of more than one
period. The Book of the Covenant — and certainly the part of it called
the Mishpatim, with the section concerning release — is among
the oldest constituents of this stratum. We should not be surprised
to come across in other parts of E notions in advance of it and nearer
to D. For another thing, *non constat* that, while we get in the Book
of the Covenant those regulations which at the time it was essential
to set forth in clear language and endow with special authority,
certain further usages were not widely recognized even then; we
shall say a little more on this below.[3]

Anyhow, there is a striking parallel to the situation we are as-
suming. According to the Book of the Covenant capital punishment is to be inflicted on a man who has sexual commerce with a
beast.[4] No mention is made of adultery. Not till the Priestly Code
and D do we find statutes directed against this crime. None the less
E is unquestionably familiar with a law imposing the death penalty
on an adulterer, in fact, a law close in terminology to D: it is God
who invokes it, in his threat to Abimelech who has taken Sarah into

[1] Cp. Ex 3.21 and Dt 15.13.   [2] Ex 21.2ff.
[3] See pp. 51, 67.   [4] Ex 22.18(19).

18

Problems of Method

his harem.[1] The phrase 'married to a husband', beᶜulath baᶜal, occurs nowhere in the Old Testament but in the story of Sarah with Abimelech and the Deuteronomic law. It is impossible to regard the lawgiver as deriving the punishability of adultery from the story. Apart from the general absurdity of such a theory, the problem in which the story is interested is the special position of Abimelech who was genuinely ignorant of Sarah's married status. But this can be a problem only where the punishability of adultery as such is fully established. Here, then, is a case where E quotes a law one might expect in the Book of the Covenant (since illicit intercourse is among the topics dealt with) but which is preserved only in D. Or more exactly, a later version is preserved, for it is demonstrable that in at least one important respect the Deuteronomic statute innovates compared with the law in E's time.[2]

A complication of a different sort is raised by the statutes the Pentateuch ostensibly derives from the exodus. As remarked above, some of the very laws which, or precursors of which, determined the construction of the exodus are based in the Pentateuch on that event. A Hebrew slave becomes free in the jubilee, 'for they are my slaves which I brought out of Egypt.'[3] It might be argued that here at least we are flying in the face of the evidence: such a law cannot have preceded the story. However, while this is true, of course, of the actual reference to the story, it is not necessarily true of the body of the statute. The Bible frequently reinterprets or supplies with a novel reason practices of long standing. In P's account of the creation God rests on the seventh day and, therefore, consecrates it for ever, an explanation recurring in one version of the Decalogue.[4] It is none the less open to us to hold that the institution of the Sabbath once existed independently of the creation story, and indeed that it had a considerable effect on the formation of the latter. An even closer analogy is provided by the derivation from the exodus of the statute enjoining the sanctification of the firstborn:[5] 'The Lord slew all the firstborn in Egypt, therefore I sacrifice all that openeth the matrix and the firstborn of

[1] Gn 20.3.
[2] See *Daube, Sin, Ignorance and Forgiveness in the Bible*, 1960, 7ff.; *The Deed and the Doer in the Bible* (Gifford Lectures Edinburgh, 1962, to be published), ch. 9, Women.
[3] Lv 25.42. [4] Gn 2.2f., Ex 20.11. [5] Ex 13.15, D.

my children I redeem.' There can be no doubt that this sacrifice not only antedates the exodus narrative but also underlies several well-known episodes in it. Significantly, in a number of cases of this kind, the aetiology of the law, from a formal point of view, is not an integral part, it could be excised without rendering the rest — formally — any less complete. The rules about the jubilee would run quite smoothly without the explanation 'for they are my slaves . . .'.

It cannot, admittedly, be repeated too often that what the authors of the epic proceeded from may not have been the statute as we have it before us today. It is in fact most unlikely that the particular concept of 'a jubilee' contributed to the narrative of the exodus. Exactly how much, and which elements, of later legislation we may carry back into an earlier era is a subject for careful inquiry. A further point is to be borne in mind. There is always a chance, even discounting aetiology, that the substance or phrasing of a law is inspired by the exodus. That may be the case, in regard to detail, even where the main idea of the law is ancient, prior to the story. Accordingly, whenever we detect a parallel between the story and a social regulation of the Pentateuch, the possibility of the story drawing on the regulation — in its present or a more primitive form — must not make us forget that of the latter drawing on the former.

As a matter of fact, I am unable to adduce any instance where such influence of the narrative on a statute is assured. Here is a case, at least, where the matter seems in the balance. The Priestly Code forbids an Israelite to rule 'with cruelty', *bepherekh*, over an Israelite slave, or — very much to the point when we look for associations with the exodus — to allow an alien (a resident alien) to do so.[1] The only other occurrences of the word in the Pentateuch are in the exodus story, where we are told twice, in successive verses, that the Egyptians made the children of Israel serve 'with cruelty'.[2] The two verses are also from P, though it should be noted that the very presence of the rare phrase is an argument for this attribution.[3] That the general object of humanity towards slaves was known to the narrators from the usage of their time is certain. The question is whether it was expressed in precisely this way or whether this is their coinage, taken over into the statutes.

[1] Lv 25.43, 46, 53.   [2] Ex 1.13f., P.   [3] Beer, op. cit., 14.

Problems of Method

There are complicating factors. The rather uncommon verb 'to rule', *radha*, employed in the legislation under discussion,[1] is not employed in the verses referring to the 'cruelty' of the Egyptians.[2] On the other hand, one of these two verses[3] contains the equally uncommon form *ᶜabhadh be*, 'to work through somebody', 'to make somebody serve', which also figures in the legislation, though not in the particular clause forbidding 'cruelty'.[4] Again, Ezekiel charges the leaders of the people: 'With force and with cruelty have ye ruled them.'[5] This is the only remaining occurrence of 'cruelty' in the Bible, and it appears in conjunction with 'to rule', exactly as in the social laws. But it is none the less possible that the prophet is chiefly inspired by a narrative source. He is speaking of the unfortunate nation at large rather than, like those laws, of an unfortunate individual. Moreover, he adds 'with force', *behozqa*, to 'with cruelty'. In the Book of Judges,[6] Jabin, king of Canaan, 'opresses' the Israelites 'with force'. The term is met in no extant statute; though, to add to the tangle, 'to oppress', *lahaṣ*, recurs not only in the exodus story[7] and other stories dependent on it[8] but also in the laws for the protection of the stranger.[9] The remark about Jabin is indeed also from the exodus scheme.[10] On the whole, it is best to keep an open mind about where 'with cruelty' originated.

[1] In all three verses, Lv 25.43, 46, 53.   [2] Ex 1.13f., P.
[3] Ex 1.14.
[4] Lv 25.39, 46: 'Thou shalt not make him serve a slave's service,' 'them (aliens) ye may make serve for ever.'
[5] Ez 34.4.
[6] 4.3. In our opinion this parallel renders objectionable any attempt to emend Ez 34.4. That the grammar of this verse gives no ground for emendation is pointed out by Cooke, *The Book of Ezekiel*, 1936, 380.
[7] Ex 3.9, E, cp. Dt 26.7 with the noun.
[8] Judg 2.18, 6.9 (direct mention of the exodus), 10.12 (direct mention in v. 11), 1 Sm 10.18 (direct mention), 2 Kgs 13.4, 22; cp. also Is 19.20, Jer 30.20, Am 6.14, Ps 56.2(1), 106.42, and the noun in Ps 42.10(9), 43.2, 44.25(24), Job 36.15.
[9] Ex 22.20(21), 23.9, Book of the Covenant, E.   [10] See above, p. 12.

III

Criteria

As a rule of thumb, dependence of the story on laws and customs may be assumed when one or more of the following three conditions are satisfied. First, the events related accord with a usage of a more or less universal character, occurring also outside Israel, in other Eastern or Mediterranean civilizations, if not even further afield. Slavery or some kind of subjugation of one person by another, restraint on ill-treatment of a slave, termination of bondage after a certain number of years, intervention by the head of a family or another near relation where the victim of a wrong cannot help himself, and more particularly the recovery of a dependant from foreign servitude and the change of allegiance resulting from it — all these usages are evidenced in many systems and at widely distant periods. It is not credible that, in Israel, the legislators had to derive them from the story. When we find them determining God's actions, the story-tellers are basing on the then prevailing social practices.

Secondly, the events related, if considered by themselves, as mere facts, have little point, or are improbable, but become significant when set against the background of the social regulations. One illustration is the haggling between Moses and Pharaoh about whether the heads of families alone might depart or whether they might take their families and cattle with them; at one point, indeed, Pharaoh is requested to provide the children of Israel with animals of his own for sacrifice.[1] Another example is the despoliation of the Egyptians by the departing Hebrews, a queer interlude which receives at least three mentions.[2] We shall devote chapters 6 and 7

[1] Ex 10.25, J.
[2] Ex 3.21f., J, 11.2f., E, 12.35f., J, possibly Gn 15.14, E.

to these episodes. We are not pronouncing on their historicity. What we are maintaining is that, in the minds of the authors, their interest lay in their connection with the rules concerning the dismissal of a slave; in the end the Egyptians are made to exercise towards the Israelites that openhandedness which law and custom enjoin on a master on that occasion. While law and custom could not have grown out of these incidents, the latter make sense as part of the construction of the exodus here postulated.

Thirdly, the terminology of the story is so deeply embedded in the social laws and customs, so basic, old, widespread in that field, that it is impossible to regard it as having originated in the story; it is the story which is indebted to the laws and customs. At the end of the foregoing chapter we concluded that the expression *be-pherekh*, 'with cruelty', cannot with confidence be assigned to this class; it is conceivable that the story comes first. There is more to be said for *laḥaṣ*, 'to oppress', also mentioned in chapter 2, being of legal provenance: it occurs in the early Book of the Covenant. As observed above, that the Book of Covenant rests its warning against 'oppression' on the experience of Egypt — 'for ye were strangers', 'for ye know the heart of a stranger' — does not prove the warnings as such to be later than the story.

However, there are obvious instances. The nouns *ʿebhedh*, 'slave', 'servant', and *ʿabhodha*, 'slave's work', 'service', and the verb *ʿabhadh*, 'to do slave's work', 'to serve', without doubt denoted a social phenomenon the narrators saw around them. In the Pentateuch this root is used of the period in Egypt some thirty times.[1] The figure, high as it is, does not, however, convey the true role of the concept. It is in the minds of the story-tellers in many more texts, for instance, when they speak of the children of Israel being 'dismissed' or 'going out' from Egypt: we shall inspect these terms below. The designation of Egypt as 'a house of slaves' — 'I am the Lord thy God which have brought thee out of the land of Egypt, out of a house of slaves' — can have come into existence only

---

[1] (1) *ʿebhedh* in Dt 5.15, 6.21, 15.15, 16.12, 24.18, 22 and in the phrase 'house of slaves' in Ex 13.3, D, 13.14, D, 20.2, P, Dt 5.6, 6.12, 7.8, 8.14, 13.6(5), 11(10); we discount Ex 5.15f., J, where 'thy slave' is the usual self-designation in talking to a king. (2) *ʿabodha* in Ex 1.14, J and P, 2.23, P, 5.9, J, 5.11, J, 6.6, P, 6.9, P, Dt 26.6. (3) *ʿabhadh* in Gn 15.13f., E, Ex 1.13f., P, 5.18, J, 6.5, P, 14.5, J, 14.12, J.

where the view of that period as one of 'slavery' was firmly established. Ancient near-Eastern documents, incidentally, also on occasion speak of redemption from a place — 'the house of so-and-so' — instead of from the master — 'the hand of so-and-so'.[1]

Or take *yashabh*, less popular with the narrators but also, as they use it, descending from legal institutions. It primarily means 'to sit', 'to dwell', 'to stay'. A derivative noun, however, *toshabh*, is specialized, signifying 'resident alien', 'sojourner', a common figure in antiquity; and in not a few passages throughout the Old Testament the verb definitely has the connotation 'to live as a subject' — be it as resident alien, hireling, slave or inferior wife. The Accadian *washabu*, too, in most cases implies dependence.[2] To give a selection, Jacob 'dwells' with Laban[3] and the captive ark with the Philistines:[4] on these more will be said in chapters 8ff. Love for Dinah induces the Schechemites to invite Jacob and his family 'to dwell' with them.[5] Judah offers 'to stay' with Joseph as slave.[6] Moses 'dwells' as a dependant with his father-in-law,[7] a Levite as a private priest with a wealthy Ephraimite.[8] As for the exodus, it should be noted that the Israelites, on immigrating in Joseph's lifetime, are allowed 'to dwell' in Goshen or Egypt,[9] surely as a kind of guest-tribe. In actual references to the deliverance, however, the verb is met only three times. As the Israelites leave, we are informed that 'the dwelling (*moshabh*, another noun from this verb) of the children of Israel who dwelt in Egypt was four hundred and thirty years . . . the selfsame day they went out'.[10] We shall presently see that 'to go out', *yaṣa³*, is associated with the liberation of a slave. Subsequently they complain: 'Would we had died in Egypt when we dwelt by the fleshpots.'[11] The usual translation is 'when we sat', but the continuation 'for ye brought us out to kill us' — with the causative of 'to go out', *hoṣi³*, 'to bring out' — suggests a

---

[1] Yaron, Revue Internationale des Droits de l'Antiquité, 3rd ser., 6, 1959, 168 n. 24.

[2] Lewy, Zeitschrift für Assyriologie 36, 1925, 149 n. 2, 159 n. 4, Goetze, Sumer 14, 1958, 30.

[3] Gn 29.14, J, 29.19, E.   [4] 1 Sm 5.7.

[5] Gn 34.10, 16, 21ff., E. In verses 16 and 21, it is true, equality seems to be stressed.

[6] Gn 44.33, J.   [7] Ex 2.21, J.

[8] Judg 17.11.   [9] Gn 45.10, 46.34, 47.4, 6, 27, J, 50.22, E.

[10] Ex 12.40f., P.   [11] Ex 16.3, P.

more pointed contrast between comfortable dependence and perilous freedom. It is relevant to recall that, in times of scarcity, the bargaining away of freedom — or part of it — in return for food is well documented in the ancient Orient.[1] The contrast recurs in the third passage, in Moses's message to the king of Edom:[2] 'We dwelt in Egypt . . . and the Lord brought us out.'

The preponderance of *ʿebhedh* and *ʿabhadh*, 'slave' and 'to serve', over *yashabh*, 'to dwell', is striking. It is explained by the concern of the story-tellers. Though the former root can be used of subjection less radical than slavery[3] and the latter can be used of slavery,[4] in general that is not the case. 'To dwell', that is, in general does not evoke the same abject status as 'slave' or 'to serve'. A Hebrew, it is ordained in P, who sells himself to a fellow-Hebrew must be treated not as 'a slave' but as 'a sojourner'.[5] Evidently a rescue by God from 'serving' was a greater thing, both in itself and in its likely effects on the consciences of those to whom it was preached, than one from 'dwelling'.

We may indeed ask why *yashabh* was employed at all. An easy way out would be to say that the verb in the three relevant passages does refer — as it can — to the lowest status, not that of a guest-tribe. But this is implausible, especially when we consider that all three passages belong to P: P is the only source in the Pentateuch mentioning the *toshabh*, the 'sojourner'. Two possibilities emerge. Either P preserves the débris of a very early tradition, which construed the exodus as the freeing of a 'sojourning' people rather than of a people 'enslaved'. (Not that the two constructions might not coexist — but we should not ascribe too much inexactitude in such matters to Old Testament writers.) Whether that would have been closer to historical facts we dare not decide. At any rate it would be understandable that the more impressive, more radical construction won the day. We incline to a second possibility, that the three allusions to a 'sojourn' are due to a view of the nation's destiny spccially favoured by P. It would lead too

---

[1] Yaron, RIDA 1959, 161ff. Cp. Gn 47.13ff., J.
[2] Nu 20.15f., JE.
[3] E.g. the verb is used of the *toshabh*, the 'sojourner', in Lv 25.40.
[4] E.g. in Gn 44.33, J, in Judah's offer just cited.
[5] Lv 25.40f. That the verb 'to serve' is here applied also to the 'sojourner' we saw in the last footnote but one.

far afield to pursue the matter further.[1] At the end of this chapter we shall cite another instance — the use of *shephaṭim*, 'judgments' — shewing that P is apt to go its own way.

That the view is not peculiar to P may be seen from an inspection of *gar*, 'to sojourn'. It is more or less synonymous with *yashabh* in one of the texts concerning the immigration of the Hebrews into Egypt.[2] They explain to Pharaoh: 'To sojourn (*gar*) we are come... now therefore let thy servants dwell (*yashabh*) in Goshen'. The verb is not met once in the actual epic of the exodus, nor is the noun *ger*, 'sojourner', 'stranger'. The latter, however, occurs in the announcement to Abraham[3] that 'thy seed will be a stranger in a land not theirs, and they shall serve them . . .'; in a Deuteronomic law[4] to the effect that an Egyptian may be received into the congregation 'because thou wast a stranger in his land'; and in reminders attached to social rulings in the Book of the Covenant, the Priestly Code and D, 'for ye were strangers in the land of Egypt.'[5] In the announcement to Abraham, the sense is technical: 'temporary, tolerated alien.' It is with this status that his descendants will start off in Egypt, but then they will be enslaved, 'they shall serve them.' The same use surely prevails in the law recommending the reception of Egyptians: 'thou wast a stranger there,' namely, before the era of oppression, the hospitality then enjoyed is to be gratefully reciprocated. The remaining passages employ 'stranger' more loosely, covering the period of oppression. Here, then, the tendency to substitute a different concept for 'slavery' extends well beyond P.

We go on to *ʿinna*, 'to afflict a dependant'. God foretells Abraham that the Egyptians will do this to the Israelites: 'Know that thy seed will be a stranger and shall serve them, and they will afflict them.'[6] The verb recurs in the story itself, where the harshness of the Egyptians is recorded, 'And they set taskmasters over them to afflict them,'[7] as well as in later texts influenced by the story.[8] Its origin in the area of social rights and duties is assured by the fact that it appears not only in the Book of the Covenant, 'Ye

[1] Interesting texts are Gn 23.4, P, Lv 25.23, 1 Chr 29.15, Ps 39.13(12).
[2] Gn 47.4,J.   [3] Gn 15.13, E.   [4] Dt 23.8(7).
[5] Ex 22.20(21), 23.9, E, LO.C. 19.34, Dt 10.19.
[6] Gn 15.13, E.   [7] Ex 1.11f., E, cp. also Dt 26.6.
[8] 2 Sm 7.10, Ps 89.23(22), 94.5, 132.1.

shall not afflict any widow or fatherless child' etc.[1] but also in two
incidents from the lives of the patriarchs with a distinctly legal
flavour. 'And Sarai afflicted Hagar', we are told, 'and she fled;'[2]
and in the course of the treaty between Jacob and Laban the latter
declares, 'If thou shalt afflict my daughters and if thou shalt take
wives besides my daughters, . . . see God is witness.'[3]

We often hear of the 'cry' of the children of Israel; the verb is
sa^caq or za^caq, the noun se^caqa.[4] It occurs in the story itself,[5]
in references to the story[6] and in other stories fashioned on the
exodus.[7] Once again, origin in social justice may be safely asserted.
In the Book of the Covenant the provisions in favour of the widow,
orphan and pledge debtor are reinforced by the warning that God
will listen to their 'cry'.[8] But, as in the case of ^cinna, 'to afflict',
what is equally suggestive is the legal or social connotation of 'to
cry' in a number of early narratives not deriving from the exodus.[9]
A person may 'cry' to the king for justice;[10] a person in distress may
'cry' for help to the king or a prophet;[11] the leader of one tribe may
'cry' to another tribe for help against an external enemy;[12] a person,
wronged, may 'cry' for redress to anyone concerned — so that a
brother, for example, may take notice.[13] Of particular interest is
Abel's blood 'crying' to God.[14] Here, where no human can exact
retribution, can act as 'recoverer of the blood', God is represented
as stepping in, much as in the exodus narrative yet, let us note
again, independently of it; it is indeed an individual, not the nation,
whose cause God maintains.

The verb $ga^>al$, 'to recover', appears twice in the exodus epic; in
God's promise to Moses, 'I will recover you with a stretched out
arm and with great judgments,' and in the song of the red sea, 'thou
in thy mercy has guided this people which thou hast recovered.'[15]

---

[1] Ex 22.21(22)f., E.   [2] Gn 16.6, J.
[3] Gn 31.50, E. We shall see, in chapter 8, pp. 65f., that the term here
approaches a somewhat specialized meaning.
[4] On the 'cry' of the Egyptians see below, p. 77.
[5] Addressed to God in Ex 2.23, P, 3.7, J, 3.9, E, 14.10, E, 14.15, J, to
Pharaoh in 5.8, J, 5.15, J.
[6] Nu 20.16, JE, Dt 26.7, Jo 24.7, Judg 10.12, 14 (cp. Is 19.20), 1 Sm
12.8, 10.
[7] Judg 3.9, 15, 4.3, 6.6f., 10.10, 12, 14, 1 Sm 7.8f., probably also 8.18.
[8] Ex 22.22(23), 26(27), E.   [9] An interesting late one in Neh 5.1, 6.
[10] 2 Sm 19.29(28), 1 Kgs 20.39, 2 Kgs 6.26, 8.3, 5.   [11] Gn 41.55, E, 2 Kgs 4.1.
[12] Jdgs 12.2.   [13] 2 Sm 13.19.   [14] Gn 4.10, J.   [15] Ex 6.6, P, 15.13, D.

27

The reason we prefer the translation 'to recover' to the usual 'to redeem' is that the element of payment, suggested by *redimere*, though certainly present in quite a few cases, is not essential to the concept. There is no trace of it in the two passages just quoted. The main idea is the getting back of a person or object into the family where there is his or its original, legitimate place, partly in the interest of the family, partly in that of the person or even the object. From Deutero-Isaiah onwards the verb, or the noun *ge᾽ulla*, 'recovery', becomes central in thought about salvation;[1] actually the 'Recoverer of Israel' is invoked in the Eighteen Benedictions.[2] The root goes back to the area of social justice. The Priestly Code and D, in legislation crystallizing very early usages, employ it in dealing with the 'recovery' of a person enslaved by an alien,[3] of a murdered relation's blood,[4] of a debt due to a relation,[5] of land sold by an impoverished person[6] and of consecrated objects.[7] Besides, the 'recoverer of blood' figures in the fictitious murder case submitted to David by the woman of Tekoah.[8] The usurper Zimri killed not only the king but all 'the kinsfolks and friends' of his house; the Hebrew for 'kinsfolks' is 'recoverers' — he left no one who could have revenged the deed.[9] Jeremiah in 587 B.C., during the siege of Jerusalem, 'recovers' his uncle's land, thus demonstrating his faith in ultimate restoration.[10] In the Book of Ruth the root occurs nearly twenty times[11] of the 'recovery' of a relation's childless widow and land. (Both in the case of Jeremiah and that of Ruth it is really a question of property which, though not yet lost to the family, would get lost but for the 'recovery'.) It cannot be the exodus that started it all off. The bards of the exodus — and indeed any who construed divine intervention as 'recovery' — availed themselves of a familiar legal concept. In fact the legal colouring

---

[1] It occurs over twenty times from Is 40 onwards, compared with a single occurrence in previous chapters, and that is 35.9, i.e. in a chapter generally considered post-exilic.

[2] Singer's Daily Prayer Book, 47; cp. Ben-Sira 51.12v (extant only in Hebrew).

[3] Lv 25.48f., 51f., 54.

[4] Nu 35.12, 19, 24f., 27, P, Dt 19.6, 12, Jo 20.3, 5, 9.   [5] Nu 5.8, P.

[6] Lv 25.24ff., 29ff.   [7] Lv 27.13, 15, 19f., 27f., 31, 33.   [8] 2 Sm 14.11.

[9] 1 Kgs 16.11. In Ez 11.15 *ge᾽ulla* signifies 'kinship' in a less pregnant sense.

[10] Jer 32.7f.

[11] 2.20, 3.9, 12 (twice), 13 (four times), 4.1, 3, 6 (five times), 7f., 14.

never fades. In Proverbs[1] we are admonished: 'Enter not into the fields of the fatherless, for their recoverer is mighty, he shall plead their cause with thee'.

Shillaḥ, 'to dismiss', 'to let go', occurs some forty times in the exodus;[2] from 'after that he will let you go',[3] through 'let my son go'[4] and 'let my people go',[5] to the second thoughts of the Egyptians after the escape, 'why have we done this, that we have let Israel go from serving us?'[6] This is legal terminology. The Book of the Covenant provides[7] that a master who ill-treats his slave, knocking out his eye or tooth, must 'let him go'. In Deuteronomy the verb signifies the 'dismissal' of a slave in the seventh year,[8] of a female captive whom the captor married but no longer desires,[9] and of a wife — divorce.[10] Outside the codes, we hear of Jacob being 'let go' by Laban.[11] We shall come back to this story in chapter 8, and to that of how the Philistines 'let go' the ark in chapters 9f.[12] Abraham 'dismisses' Hagar,[13] and we may compare Moses's 'dismissal', *shilluḥim*, of Zipporah, in which clause the noun may well hint at a divorce.[14] Abraham also pays off and 'dismisses' the sons of his concubines,[15] and again we may compare a passage with the noun *shilluḥim*, where it denotes a kind of dowry for a daughter.[16] According to Gordon,[17] *shilluḥim* in the sense of 'dowry' probably derives from a root *tlḥ* preserved in Ugaritic. Even should this be so, once the shift to the present consonants had taken place, people must have connected the word with *shillaḥ*. (Whatever the ultimate etymology of *parricidas* may turn out to be, as far as historical Roman law is concerned it would not do to neglect the popular opinions entertained by the jurists.) God 'dismisses', drives out, Adam from Eden, his first home.[18] Several narratives mention the

---

[1] 23.10f.
[2] Ex 3.20, J, 4.21, J, 4.23, J, 5.1, E, 5.2 (twice), E, 6.1, J, 6.11, P, 7.2, P, 7.14, J, 7.16, J, 7.26(8.1)f., J, 8.4(8), J, 8.16(20), J, 8.24(28)f., J, 8.28(32), J, 9.1f., J, 9.7, J, 9.13, J, 9.17, J, 9.28, J, 9.35, E, 10.3f., J, 10.7, J, 10.10, J, 10.20, E, 10.27, E, 11.1 (twice), E, 11.10, P, 12.33, J, 13.15, D, 13.17, E, 14.5, J.
[3] Ex 3.20, J.   [4] Ex 4.23, J.   [5] Ex 5.1, E.   [6] Ex 14.5, J.
[7] Ex 21.26f., E. The verses form part of the Mishpatim.
[8] Dt 15.12f., 18.   [9] Dt 21.14.   [10] Dt 22.19, 29, 24.1, 3f.
[11] Gn 30.25, J, 31.27, J, 31.42, E.   [12] 1 Sm 5.10f., 6.2f., 6, 8.
[13] Gn 21.14, E.   [14] Ex 18.2, E.   [15] Gn 25.6, J or P.   [16] 1 Kgs 9.16.
[17] *Ugaritic Manual*, 1955, 328, 336 (Glossary nos. 1835, 2030).
[18] Gn 3.23, J.

'dismissal' of an enemy in one's power.[1] Of the prophets, Jeremiah uses the word of the 'dismissal' and re-enslavement of fellow-Hebrews under Zedekiah, referring to the codes.[2] Trito-Isaiah preaches that a true fast involves the 'dismissal' of the down-trodden.[3] Cyrus, says Deutero-Isaiah,[4] will 'let go' the exiles; post-exilic writers describe national restoration as a 'dismissal' from fetters;[5] and Ezekiel represents God as 'letting go', setting free, the souls caught by false prophets.[6] Both Deutero-Isaiah and Jeremiah speak of Israel's 'dismissal', divorce, by God, her husband.[7] In one passage in Jeremiah the people's 'dismissal' by God, while implying a rejection, does not allude to divorce; probably the prophet is thinking of renunciation of a dependant, a child or the like.[8]

The field of *garash* or *geresh*, 'to expel', overlaps with that of *shillaḥ*; but whereas the latter often refers to friendly release, the former is invariably a hostile act. It figures only three times in the exodus, being justified essentially by the final plague: the Israelites are now looked on as such a source of ill-luck that their masters cannot get rid of them too soon.[9] Ancient anti-semitism made good use of this motif.[10] In two texts the verb is paired off with *shillaḥ*. One is: 'Through a strong hand shall he (be compelled to) let them go and with a strong hand shall he (be compelled to) expel them out of his land.'[11] The other will be considered in detail in chapter 7: 'As one would let go a slave-wife shall he surely expel you hence.'[12] Then there is the notice that the departing Israelites had no time to wait for their dough to be leavened, 'for they were expelled from Egypt'.[13] In the Priestly Code and Ezekiel the verb is used of a divorcee.[14] It recurs, together with *shillaḥ*, in the story of Hagar's ejection by Abraham,[15] and in that of Adam's from Eden.[16] Cain is 'expelled' from his soil for his murder.[17] The family of Gaal

---

[1] Judg 1.25, 2 Sm 3.24, 1 Kgs 20.42.   [2] Jer 34.9ff., 14, 16.
[3] Is 58.6.   [4] Is 45.13.
[5] Jer 50.33, Zech 9.11. Jer 50.34 we quoted above, for *gaʾal*, 'to recover'.
[6] Ez 13.20.   [7] Is 50.1, Jer 3.1, 8.
[8] Jer 15.1; cp. Gn 3.23, J, Adam's 'dismissal', quoted above.
[9] See particularly Ex 11.1, E.   [10] Josephus, C. Ap. 1.26, 229ff.
[11] Ex 6.1, J.   [12] Ex 11.1, E.   [13] Ex 12.39, J.
[14] Lv 21.7, 14, 22.13, Nu 30.10(9), P, Ez 44.22.
[15] Gn 21.10, E; verse 14, E, with *shillaḥ*, was quoted above.
[16] Gn 3.24, J; *shillaḥ* in verse 23, J.   [17] Gn 4.14, J.

is 'expelled', exiled, from Shechem for political reasons.[1] The young Jephtha, son of a concubine, is 'expelled' by the legitimate heirs.[2] David, persecuted by Saul, suspects that enemies have contrived to 'expel' him from his country, drive him into exile.[3] Solomon 'expels' Abiathar from a hereditary priestly office;[4] and Jehoshaphat resists the Ammonites and Moabites, come to 'expel' the people of Judah from their inheritance.[5] To turn to the prophets, they declaim against the unjust 'expulsion' of a man from his possession;[6] and sinful Ephraim is to be 'expelled' from the house of God.[7] Finally, in Job, Proverbs and Psalms we hear of unworthy people or lunatics being 'expelled', banished, from society or a country.[8]

The children of Israel *yaṣaʾ*, 'go out', from Egypt some thirty-five times,[9] from the promise to Abraham,[10] 'Know that thy seed shall be a stranger and shall serve them, and afterwards shall they go out with great substance,' to the record of its fulfilment,[11] 'The selfsame day went out all the hosts from Egypt,' and subsequent reminiscences. This 'going out' is to be commemorated by ceremonies.[12] Future redemption is described by the same term.[13] The term is legal, borrowed by the story-tellers. The Book of the Covenant lays down[14] that a slave is to 'go out' in the seventh year unless he waives this right; and a daughter sold by her father has special privileges in regard to 'going out'. According to the Priestly Code, property may 'go out' in the jubilee.[15] Deuteronomy uses the verb in a provision concerning a slave's waiver of his release;[16] also in connection with divorce, of a woman whom her husband 'dis-

---

[1] Judg 9.41.　　[2] Judg 11.2, 7.　　[3] 1 Sm 26.19.　　[4] 1 Kgs 2.27.
[5] 2 Chr 20.11.
[6] Ez 45.9, Mi 2.9; the latter passage conceivably refers to divorce.
[7] Hos 9.15.
[8] Job 30.5, Prv 22.10, Ps 34.1 (inscription). The last-mentioned text refers to the incident recorded in 1 Sm 21.14ff.
[9] Gn 15.14, E, Ex 11.8, J, 12.31, E, 12.41, P, 14.8, J, 16.1, P, 19.1, P, Nu 1.1, P, 9.1, P, 11.20, JE, 22.5, JE, 22.11, JE, 26.4, P, 33.3, P, 33.38, P, Dt 4.45f., 9.7, 11.10, 23.5(4), 24.9, 25.17, Jo 2.10, 5.4ff., 1 Kgs 6.1, 8.9 (equals 2 Chr 5.10), 2 Kgs 21.15, Jer 7.25, Ps 68.8(7), 81.6(5), 105.38, 114.1.
[10] Gn 15.13f., E.　　　　　　[11] Ex 12.41, P.
[12] Ex 13.3f., D, 13.8, D, 23.15, E, 34.18, JE, Dt 16.3, 6.
[13] Is 49.9, 52.12, 55.12, Jer 51.45, Mi 7.15, Hag 2.5.
[14] Ex 21.2ff., 7, 11, E — all part of the Mishpatim.
[15] Lv 25.30f.　　　　　　　　[16] Dt 15.16.

misses', *shillaḥ*, and who thereupon 'goes out of his house'.[1] Accadian *waṣu* may be compared.[2]

When we turn to the causative of *yaṣaʾ*, however, *hoṣiʾ*, 'to cause to go out', 'to bring out', with the Israelites as object, we reach a point where the story has developed its own momentum. This form is not traceable, outside the exodus complex, in early Biblical social practices. To be sure, the corresponding Accadian *shuṣu* is technical for 'redemption', and quite likely *hoṣiʾ* had the same force before the exodus story was composed.[3] None the less the figures shew that its role in the Bible is not a reflection of the role it played in the social-legal field: it is due to the story itself.

Hoṣiʾ is even more frequent than *yaṣaʾ*. It occurs some fifty-five times in the exodus and subsequent references to it;[4] in addition, about ten times where commemoration of the exodus is enjoined;[5] in addition, some fifteen times where the exodus serves to underline the bindingness of God's commandments on the Israelites;[6] in addition, a few times in Ezekiel's prophecies of future salvation;[7] in addition, half a dozen times or so in the Psalmist's description of salvation, national or individual;[8] and in addition, in a passage probably modelled on the exodus, where God 'brings out' Abraham from Ur.[9] What about social legislation? *Hoṣiʾ* never occurs in

---

[1] Dt 24.2. In Jer 15.2 also 'to go out' is the other side of 'to dismiss'; see above, on 15.1.

[2] Code of Hammurabi 172, Assyrian Laws 34, 37, 46.

[3] See Yaron, RIDA 1959, 160ff., and especially 165 n. 15 for the relevance to the exodus story.

[4] Ex 3.10ff., E, 6.6f., P, 6.13, P, 6.26f., P, 7.4f., P, 12.17, P, 12.42, P, 12.51, P, 14.11, J, 16.3, P, 16.6, P, 16.32, P, 18.1, E, 32.11f., E, Lv 26.45, Nu 20.16, JE, 23.22, JE, 24.8, J, Dt 1.27, 7.19, 9.12, 26, 28f., 29.24(25), Jo 24.5f., Judg 2.12, 6.8, 1 Sm 12.8, 1 Kgs 8.16 (equals 2 Chr 6.5), 21, 51, 53, 9.9 (equals 2 Chr 7.22), Jer 31.31(32), 32.21, Ez 20.6, 9f., 14, 22, Dan 9.15, Ps 68.7(6), 105.37, 136.11.

[5] Ex 13.3, 9, 14, 16, D, Lv 23.43, Dt 6.21, 23, 16.1, 26.8; Dt 6.23 might be taken under the next group, we place it here because of its closeness to Ex 13.14, D.

[6] Ex 20.2, P, 29.46, P, Lv 19.36, 22.33, 26.13, Nu 15.41, P, Dt 4.20, 37, 5.6, 6.12, 7.8, 8.14, 13.6(5), 11(10), Jer 7.22, 11.4.

[7] Ez 14.22 (Hophal, the passive), 20.34, 34.13, 38.4, 38.8 (Hophal again), possibly also Jer 51.10.

[8] Ps 25.17, 31.5(4), 37.6 (?), 66.12, 107.14, 28, 142.8(7), also 2 Sm 22.49.

[9] Gn 15.7, D (?), cited in Neh 9.7. In Jo 6.22f. they 'bring out' to safety Rahab and her family, for her services to the spies; but there is no reason to assume dependence on the exodus narrative.

the substantive portion, though the Priestly Code bases on God's 'bringing out' of the Israelites the prohibition of usury among Hebrews[1] and the release of a Hebrew slave in the jubilee,[2] D, in the Ten Commandments, the Sabbatical rest of a slave,[3] and Jeremiah the release of a Hebrew slave at the end of seven years.[4] In Ezra *hoṣiʾ* signifies 'to divorce', with the foreign wives as object.[5]

Hoṣiʾ, then, is prevalent in all thinking about the exodus and in the reasons the Pentateuch gives for social laws; it is not to be found in the substantive part of any of these laws — nor, it is worth noting, in any stories (except Ezra) with a legal flavour not derived from the exodus. Evidently, it owes its prominence to the enormous importance the narrators attached to the saving activity of God, be he acting in person or — as some texts have it — through Moses (e.g. 'I will send thee unto Pharaoh that thou mayest bring out my people')[6] or Moses and Aaron (e.g. 'These are they to whom the Lord spoke, Bring out my people of Egypt').[7] The public was to be made conscious, by constant reminders, that their fathers did not merely 'go out', but that God 'brought them out': hence the narrators were not content with the simple form, they introduced the causative and indeed favoured it. This emphasis is not to be expected in the formulation of ancient usages. It was a genuine contribution of the *kerygma* which subsequently, to be sure, did add to the sanctity of social rights and duties; in the final system, the 'bringing out' by God became their *raison d'être*. In a way, the case of *hoṣiʾ* provides a check of our observations regarding those terms — like the simple *yaṣaʾ*, 'to go out' — for which we are indeed claiming direct descent, faithful adoption, from social regulations. The distribution of those terms over various settings is quite different.

It is, incidentally, from *yaṣaʾ* that the first member of the post-

---

[1] Lv 25.38.
[2] Lv 25.42, 55; maybe Lv 19.36, quoted above, among the references to the bindingness of the laws at large, belongs rather to this narrower category of social laws.
[3] Dt 5.15.   [4] Jer 34.13.
[5] 10. 3, 19; see Yaron, Revue Internationale des Droits de l'Antiquité, 3rd ser., 4, 1957, 120.
[6] Ex 3.10ff., E, 14.11, J, Dt 9.12.
[7] Ex 6.13, 26f., 16.3, P; in 16.6, P, God's 'bringing out' is contrasted to that by Moses and Aaron.

Biblical technical expression *yeṣi'ath miṣrayim*, 'the exodus from Egypt' is derived.[1] The Old Testament has no noun for the exodus; and the extreme rarity of *exodos* in this sense in the Septuagint suggests that by the time of this translation the expression discussed had not yet established itself. It marks a decisive step from thinking about that event in concrete terms towards a historical-theological concept. Awareness of the step is indicated by the fact that, though the Old Testament offers several nouns which might have done, a new one was chosen.

Like *yaṣa'*, 'to go out', though more rarely, *halakh*, 'to go', refers to what the Israelites wish to do and in the end are able to do;[2] and in several passages, like *yaṣa'*, it corresponds to a *shillaḥ*, 'dismissal', on the part of Pharaoh.[3] It is certainly less pregnant than *yaṣa'*, but there are enough texts to shew that it, too, may have legal overtones.

In the story of Jacob, to be discussed in chapter 8, his 'going' corresponds to Laban's 'dismissing', 'let me go that I may go to my place and my country,'[4] and in that of the ark, to be discussed in chapters 9f., the ark 'goes' as the Philistines 'dismiss' it; on this occasion the precedent of the exodus is actually mentioned.[5] Again, Abraham is given back his wife by the king of Egypt and allowed or urged 'to go'.[6] Isaac, having become too strong, is urged by Abimelech 'to go' from his domain.[7] Moses 'goes' from Jethro who had taken him in.[8] The Edomite Hadad, an honoured guest in Egypt, asks the king 'to dismiss' him and to be allowed 'to go'.[9] Hagar 'goes', being 'dismissed' and 'expelled' by Abraham.[10] Tamar 'goes' from her father-in-law's family to live with her own.[11] An unfaithful concubine 'goes' from her husband to live with her own family.[12] A wife whom her husband 'dismissed', divorced,

---

[1] See e.g. Sanctification (Kiddush) of Sabbath Evening, Singer's Prayer Book, 124, Passover Haggadah, Goldschmidt, Die Pessach-Haggada, 1936, 38.

[2] Ex 3.21, J, 12.31, E, 12.32, J; In connection with the temporary leave to 'go' and sacrifice, Ex 3.18f., J, 5.3, J, 5.8, J and E, 8.23(27)f., J, 10.8, J, 10.11, J, 10.24, J, 10.26, J. In the last-mentioned verse it is the cattle that 'goes'; on this question see below, ch. 6, pp. 50f.

[3] Ex 8.24(28), J, 10.9, J (cp. v. 10, J), also 3.21, J, as we shall see in ch. 7, p. 57, from a comparison with Dt 15.13 and 1 Sm 6.3.

[4] Gn 30.25, J, 30.26, E, 31.30, E (*shillaḥ* in v. 27, J).

[5] 1 Sm 6.6, 8.   [6] Gn 12.19, J.   [7] Gn 26.16, J.   [8] Ex 4.18f., J.

[9] 1 Kgs 11.21f.   [10] Gn 21.14, E.   [11] Gn 38.11, J.   [12] Judg 19.2.

'goes' from him to re-marry.[1] An adulteress 'goes' after her lovers and then, disappointed, 'goes' to return to her husband.[2] Before the army joins battle, certain categories of men are called on 'to go' and return home.[3] Apostates 'go' and serve other gods.[4] In the restored Zion, the prophet announces,[5] there will be peace and joy 'and the recovered ones shall go'; the phrase is paired off with 'and the ransomed of the Lord shall return'.

To be sure, despite all this evidence and more of the same kind, we must be careful. *Halakh* is very common in very many areas of activity. It may indeed, like its English equivalent, signify activity *per se*, introducing another more specific verb. The verse in which Moses asks 'to go' from Jethro opens, 'And he went (scil. from his meeting with God at the burning bush) and returned to Jethro', then it goes on, 'and he said to him, I would go, I pray thee, and return to my brethren.'[6] If we find the children of Israel wishing 'to go' from Egypt, we also find Pharaoh telling them: 'Go and work.'[7] Still, it is safe to assume that the narrators of the exodus did know, and were guided by, relevant uses of the verb in social laws and customs.

Lastly, for *dan*, 'to judge', and the noun *shephatim*, 'judgments', derived from a different root. *Dan* occurs only in one reference to the exodus, in God's promise to Abraham, already quoted in part because it contains *yaṣaʾ*, 'to go out': 'Know that thy seed will be a stranger and shall serve them ... and also the nation whom they shall serve will I judge, and afterwards shall they go out with great substance.'[8] The deliverance is clearly thought of as a legal process; and it may be noted that *dan* pre-eminently signifies justice for an individual or nation in a subordinate state. The childless Rachel calls her handmaid Bilha's son — who will count as Rachel's — Dan:[9] 'God hath judged me and hath also heard my voice'. (The miserable appeals to God, in line with what we said above concerning 'the cry'.) 'Judge in the morning',

---

[1] Dt 24.2, Jer 3.1. [2] Hos 2.7(5), 9(7), 15(13); cp. Jer 2.25.
[3] Dt 20.5ff.
[4] Dt 17.3, 29.17(18), 25(26), Jo 23.16, 1 Kgs 9.6, Jer 25.6, 35.15. In 1 Sm 26.19 David's enemies are out to drive him into exile, into attachment to a foreign community, so that he must 'go and serve other gods'.
[5] Is 35.9, a post-exilic section. [6] Ex 4.18, J.
[7] Ex 5.18, J and E. [8] Gn 15.14, E. [9] Gn 30.6, E.

Jeremiah exclaims,[1] 'and save the spoiled from the hand of the oppressor.' 'The Lord shall judge his people when their power is gone,' we read in Deuteronomy.[2]

However, there is a curious twist about *dan* in the reference to the exodus. With the exception of a line in Psalms[3] this is the only time the verb means 'to judge adversely', 'to punish'. Usually it means 'to help a person to his right' or at least it is neutral. Quite likely the particular nuance in the passage under review is due to the author himself; he did not find it in earlier laws and customs. As to his motive, we shall make a guess presently, when we discuss *shephaṭim*.

In four texts, all belonging to P, God is described as executing 'judgments' or 'great judgments' in Egypt. Two contain promises of deliverance: 'And I will bring you out from under the burdens of the Egyptians and I will save you from their service and I will recover you with a stretched out arm and great judgments', and again, 'And I will lay my hand upon Egypt and I will bring out mine armies, my people the children of Israel, from the land of Egypt with great judgments.'[4] In the third passage God announces the slaying of the firstborn, ending with 'and against all the gods of Egypt will I execute judgments'.[5] The fourth is dependent on the third. It occurs in an itinerary of the journeyings of the Israelites: 'On the morrow of the passover the children of Israel went out with a high hand. And the Egyptians buried all their firstborn which the Lord had smitten among them, and upon their gods the Lord executed judgments.'[6] Obviously P accepts fully the construction of the exodus on legal lines. Such proclamations should not, as is commonly done, be dismissed as mere rhetoric: they testify to a profound influence of that basic view of the event. Significantly the first passage contains the verbs *hoṣi᾽*, 'to bring out', and *ga᾽al*, 'to recover', as well as the noun *ᶜabhodha*, 'service', 'slavery', the second *hoṣi᾽*, 'to bring out', and the fourth *yaṣa᾽*, 'to go out'.

---

[1] 21.12.

[2] 32.36. See also Is 3.13, Jer 5.28, 22.16, 30.13, Ps 9.9(8), 54.3(1), 72.2, Prv 31.9; and indeed Ec 6.10 saying that the weak — man — cannot insist on justice against the strong — God. The use of the noun *dayyan*, 'judge', is closely parallel: 1 Sm 24.15, Ps 68.6(5).

[3] 110.6.   [4] Ex 6.6, 7.4, P.   [5] Ex 12.12, P.

[6] Nu 33.3f., JE having gone through the hands of P.

At the same time, *shephaṭim* is found nowhere else in the Pentateuch, and practically only in Ezekiel in the rest of the Old Testament.[1] It follows that the term is not borrowed from social practice; it is a fresh coinage, expressing a variation of the main idea peculiar to P and Ezekiel. In chapter 1 we remarked that in the social order back of the exodus story, essentially the same principles applied to enslavement and murder. In either case it was a question of preserving the integrity of a family and providing security for any member; in either case, therefore, the nearest relative would 'recover' the person lost, by freeing him if enslaved, by taking vengeance for him if murdered. In general the narrators of the exodus speak chiefly — though, to be sure, without overmuch precision — in terms of the former kind of intervention: 'Let my son go.' This seems the original scheme. The 'judgments' introduced by P seem designed to stress the latter kind. The Egyptians had been guilty of much killing — God now exacts retribution. The connection with the final plague and a triumph over the Egyptian gods strongly supports this explanation. So does Ezekiel's use of the term. We may particularly notice a prophecy that God 'will execute judgments in Egypt', among which will figure the putting to the sword of their young men and the destruction of their false gods.[2] At one time there probably were more detailed accounts of God's overthrow of the enemy's gods; the monster 'Rahab' may have played a part — it sometimes stands for Egypt.[3]

Dan, 'to judge', employed in the sense 'to judge adversely', 'to punish', may well be attributable to the same school. At first sight, since God promises Abraham that his descendants 'will go out with great substance', one might perhaps infer that *dan* envisages the enforcement of a generous release. We shall indeed come back to the phrase 'with great substance' in discussing such release. But on closer inspection it is clear that the promise distinguishes between the 'judging' which will come first and the 'going out' which will result from it: 'and also the nation whom they serve will I judge and afterwards shall they go out with great substance.' It does look

---

[1] Ten times; outside Ezekiel only in Prv 19.29 and 2 Chr 24.24.
[2] Ez 30.13ff.
[3] Is 30.7, 51.9, Ps 87.4. In Job 26.12 God 'smiteth through', *maḥaṣ*, Rahab; in Nu 24.8, J, he is praised as 'bringing out' Israel from Egypt and 'smiting through' the nations that aggrieve it. See also below, p. 84.

as if *dan*, like *shephaṭim*, referred to the slaying of the firstborn. The only other text in the Bible where the verb signifies 'to judge adversely' runs:[1] 'He shall judge among the heathens, he shall have his fill of dead bodies.' It is worth pointing out that part of the verse from Genesis with *dan*, though not the part with *dan*, is generally given to P. Maybe P's contribution does include *dan*.

It is in all four sources of the Pentateuch that we find the exodus conceived as an application of social usages. Of the relevant texts cited in this chapter, it is usual to assign

(1) to J: Gn 45.10, 46.34, 47.4, 6, 27, Ex 1.14, 3.7, 18ff., 4.21, 23, 5.3, 8f. (with E), 11, 15, 18, 6.1, 7.14, 16, 26f.(8.1f.), 8.4(8), 16 (20), 23(27)ff., 28(32), 9.1f., 7, 13, 17, 28, 10.3f., 7ff., 24ff., 11.8, 12.32f., 35f., 39, 14.5, 8, 11f., 15, Nu 24.8;

(2) to E: Gn 15.13f. (with P), 50.22, Ex 1.11f., 3.9ff., 5.1f., 8 (with J), 9.35, 10.20, 27, 11.1ff., 12.31, 13.17, 14.10, 18.1, 22.20(21), 23.9, 15, 32.11f.;

(3) to JE: Ex 34.18, Nu 11.20, 20.15f., 22.5, 11, 23.22;

(4) To P: Gn 15.13f. (with E), Ex 1.13f., 2.23, 6.5ff., 9, 11, 13, 26f., 7.2, 4f., 11.10, 12.12, 17, 40ff., 51, 16.1, 3, 6, 32, 19.1, 20.2, 29.46, Lv 19.34, 36, 22.33, 23.43, 25.38, 42, 55, 26.13, 45, Nu 1.1, 9.1, 15.41, 26.4, 33.3f., 38;

(5) to D: Gn 15.7 (?), Ex 13.3f., 8f., 14ff., 15.13 — and, of course, there are all the quotations from Deuteronomy, 1.27, 4.20, 37, 45f., 5.6, 15, 6.12, 21, 23, 7.8, 19, 8.14, 9.7, 12, 26, 28f., 10.19, 11.10, 13.6(5), 11(10), 15.15, 16.1, 3, 6, 12, 23.5(4), 8(7), 24.9, 18, 22, 25.17, 26.6ff., 29.24(25).

In fact, seeing that this conception has lost little of its vitality by the era of the New Testament and the Rabbis, the probability is that it held sway, without interruption, throughout the entire Biblical epoch. No doubt there was constant cross-fertilization between the legal ideas and the epic.

[1] Ps 110.6.

IV

Captives Abroad

Biblical legislation does not deal with a Hebrew enslaved abroad: that might have been academic. We do find plenty of legislation about Hebrew slaves at home; and, significantly, in the matter of redemption — regulated in the Priestly Code — a distinction is made between a Hebrew slave in the hand of another Hebrew and one in the hand of a resident alien. It is only the latter whom his family has the right and duty to 'recover'.[1] There can be no doubt that rescue of a relation enslaved abroad was the done thing, whenever practicable, at least as much as rescue of one on Israelite territory. When Lot was taken prisoner by the invaders of Sodom, Abraham at once pursued them and saved him.[2] Nehemiah bought off Jews 'who had sold themselves to the nations'[3] — meaning to heathens in and around Judaea and possibly even in Persia. According to the Code of Hammurabi,[4] if a person taken captive abroad while on an official mission is ransomed by a merchant, in the last resort the king will be responsible for the latter's reimbursement. The basic design of the exodus, the children of Israel's rescue by their God from a strange land, conforms to an important reality in the ancient world.

Slavery abroad was often the result of war, nearly always where a whole group became slaves. The subjection of the Israelites by the Egyptians, though not a result of war, takes place in order to prevent them from joining an enemy.[5] Again, for obvious reasons, it was common for a protector at home to use the services of a messenger to negotiate with or put pressure on the captive's master abroad. The Spartans and Philip of Macedonia sent envoys to the

[1] Lv 25.39ff., 47ff.
[3] Neh 5.8.   [4] Par. 32.

[2] Gn 14.12ff., special source.
[5] Ex 1.10, J.

39

Athenians to ransom prisoners, and the Athenians sent one to Philip.[1] That God, himself outside Egypt, at the burning bush, should send Moses[2] accords with the normal procedure in these affairs. So does the version which makes God deliver the Israelites through an angel: 'And when we cried unto the Lord, he heard our voice and sent an angel and brought us out of Egypt.'[3]

Envoys were, of course, carefully selected for their distinction and fitness for the task[4] — a point to be borne in mind when we hear of Moses's hesitation. A minimum age was sometimes required; Moses's eighty years, and Aaron's eighty-three, 'when they spake unto Pharaoh'[5] may have to do with this.[6] Jeremiah, when first called, considers himself too young to be God's messenger.[7] Frequently an embassy consisted of several persons: the dispatch of Moses and Aaron jointly is nothing out of the ordinary. As to credentials, in general an envoy needed them only vis-à-vis the party with whom he had to negotiate; and Moses and Aaron do produce theirs before Pharaoh.[8] However, where the mission was to bring a prisoner back from abroad, naturally, they were needed also vis-à-vis the latter. He too had to be convinced of the envoy's authority and indeed to assent to his action. The law of Gortyn refers to the redemption of a captive 'at his request'.[9] Hence the elaborate legitimation of Moses in the eyes of the Israelites, hence the vital importance of their trust in him.[10] When we are told how God foresees that, if faced by war, the freed slaves would return to Egypt, or how on occasion they do wish themselves back to the fleshpots,[11] that reflects a dilemma far from theoretical in antiquity — or even today. We shall quote below Biblical laws envisaging a slave's waiver of his right to freedom after a number of years.[12]

This is not the place to go into the Old Testament theology of the intermediary; as is well known, according to one school of thought the insertion of an angel between God and the people is to

---

[1] Thucydides 4.41, 3f., Demosthenes, Philip's Letter 3.159, Aeschines, Embassy 15; see Phillipson, *International Law and Custom of Ancient Rome and Greece*, 1911, 2, 260.
[2] Ex 3, J and E.   [3] Nu 20.16, JE.   [4] Phillipson, 1, 324.
[5] Ex 7.7, P.   [6] So why grumble about modern gerontocracies?
[7] Jer 1.6. Cp. 1 Kgs 3.7.   [8] E.g. Ex 7.8ff., P.
[9] 1.6, 48, *kelomeno*.   [10] Ex 3ff., J and E.   [11] Ex 13.17, E, 16.3, P, etc.
[12] Ex 21.5f., E, Dt 15.16f.; see pp. 48f.

be regretted, indeed, a punishment for their sinfulness.[1] The opposition between the two views lasts into Rabbinic times. As may be expected, in the Passover eve liturgy the emphasis is on God's direct intervention.[2] At any rate, from Jesus sent by God to save mankind, from his legitimation, or refusal to furnish legitimation, before adversaries and followers, from the insistence on the necessity of belief in him, one line of many — some of them no doubt far more important — leads back across the centuries to the practices of international commerce in the matter of prisoners of war.

[1] Very pronounced in Ex 33.2ff., J, where God promises to send an angel and to lead the people into a land flowing with milk and honey — 'and when the people heard these evil tidings they mourned'.

[2] See Daube, *The New Testament and Rabbinic Judaism*, 325ff.

V

A Change of Master

Among the major motifs directly associated with the application to the exodus of social laws and customs is that of a change of master. A person enslaved — whether at home or abroad — and redeemed by a relation became that relation's slave, though it would ordinarily be a milder and preferable kind of subjection.[1] This was the case not only in the Hebrew system[2] but in many others of antiquity. Under the law of Gortyn already quoted a ransomed captive belonged to the ransomer till reimbursement. God's demand to Pharaoh 'Let my son go that he may serve me',[3] which in the form 'Let my people go that they may serve me' is repeated over and over again,[4] is in precise accordance with usage from real life. The technical force of 'to let go' and 'to serve' was noticed in chapter 3. On the first occasion the demand is preceded by a formal statement of title: 'My firstborn son is Israel.'[5] The attribute 'firstborn', besides being wanted as a basis for the threat to the firstborn of Pharaoh,[6] may well add to the substance of the claim: here is a very close relationship, where the highest degree of loyalty may be expected of the protector, and where his opponent is grievously in the wrong.

Sometimes, quite possibly, the Israelites are thought of less as slaves to be rescued by a relation than as property withheld from its original owner and to be regained by him. That is the impression created by a passage like 'And I will take you to me for a people, and you shall know that I am the Lord your God who brought you out from under the hands of the Egyptians'.[7] The principle of a

---

[1] Cp. Yaron, RIDA 1959, 167. [2] Lv 25.47ff.
[3] Ex 4.23, J. [4] Ex 7.16, 26(8.1), 8.16(20), 9.1, 13, 10.3, J.
[5] Ex 4.22, J. [6] Ex 4.23, J. [7] Ex 6.7, P.

change of master would play the same role on this basis as on the other: the loss of inherited property affected the integrity of a family much as the loss of a member. According to Hebrew legislation, if land had fallen to a stranger, the original owner or his kinsmen had the right and duty to redeem it — upon which it belonged to the person who had regained it for the family.[1] Above, in discussing 'recovery', we mentioned the famous gesture of Jeremiah who redeemed his uncle's estate during the siege of Jerusalem, as well as Boaz's redemption of Ruth and the estate going with her. Jeremiah and Boaz saved the property and the childless widow from outside domination; instead it came under theirs.[2] Whether God acts as the mighty relation and protector of the people or as their original legitimate owner, the result of their deliverance must be the substitution of his rule for Pharaoh's.

The formula on Pharaoh's side which corresponds to God's demand is: 'Go, serve the Lord.'[3] 'To go' — to leave the master, 'to serve' — to be or become somebody else's slave. Pharaoh is consenting to the change of ruler, the transfer of the Israelites from his service to that of God. True, in some if not all of these texts 'to serve' primarily envisages an act of worship, the offer of a sacrifice; and at least on the earlier occasions Pharaoh has in mind a merely temporary removal of his slaves. But this does not affect the main idea.

How powerful the motif was may be seen from the way it is introduced where God's title over the people, his authority, is to be stressed. The Ten Commandments open 'I am the Lord thy God which have brought thee out of the land of Egypt, out of a house of slaves': that act, which established God's mastery in the place of that of their foreign oppressors, lends validity to his decrees. Or to take P, where this basis of the people's obligation towards God is no less clear:[4] 'I will be your God and you shall be my people. I am the Lord your God which brought you out of the land of Egypt, from being slaves to them, and I broke the bands of your yoke and made you go upright.' In the call of Moses, the

---

[1] Lv 25.25ff.
[2] Jer 32.6ff., Ru 2.20ff. As pointed out above, the property in these two cases was not yet lost, it was threatening to get lost.
[3] Ex 10.8, 11, 24, J, 12.31, E, 12.32, J.   [4] Lv 26.12f.

change of master sealed at Sinai is the very sign of the genuineness of his mission: 'and this shall be a token unto thee that I have sent thee, when thou hast brought out the people from Egypt, ye shall serve God upon this mountain.'[1] Once again, by 'to serve' may well be contemplated a sacrifice — we do hear of one in connection with the promulgation of the Book of the Covenant.[2] The sequence 'to bring out from Egypt' — 'to serve God' remains no less significant. The final entry of the people into God's service at this place will prove him to have initiated here their reclamation from foreign yoke through Moses.[3]

In chapter 2 we remarked that much social legislation in the Pentateuch is reinforced by reminders of the exodus or even represented as a consequence. It will not surpise that the change of master is prominent in this connection. Hebrew slaves are to be treated well and not to remain in subjection for good, 'for they are my slaves whom I brought out of the land of Egypt.'[4] So as a result of God's intervention the children of Israel, from being slaves to the Egyptians, became slaves to God — in analogy to ancient social usage; and now the social protection given by the law is rested on that change of master, on the Israelites having passed under divine rule which, essentially, precludes any other.

New deliverances proclaimed by the prophets are equally dominated by the motif. 'Fear not', we read in Deutero-Isaiah, 'for I have recovered thee, I have called thee by thy name, thou art mine.'[5] Or in Jeremiah: 'I will acknowledge them that are carried away captive of Judah . . . and they shall be my people and I will be their God.'[6] Actually, the motif retains all its vitality both in

---

[1] Ex 3.12, E. [2] Ex 24.5, E.

[3] Though the fulfilment of the sign lies in the future, it is accepted by Moses at once: cp. 1 Sm 2.34, 2 Kgs 19.29 (equals Is 37.30), Jer 44.29. Very likely, initially, 'the sign of Jonah' spoken of in Matthew and Luke meant the prediction in Jonah 3.4, 'Yet forty days and Nineveh shall be overthrown.' In Mt 16.4 this sense is still the most plausible. In Mt 12.39ff., verse 40 attempts a — secondary — explanation, in Lk 11.29ff. verse 30 another one. But for these two verses, the original sense would fit quite well even in these pericopes. The peculiarity of Jonah's prediction is, of course, that as the Ninevites accept it, God does not let it come true.

[4] Lv 25.42, 55.

[5] Is 43.1. For 'to call' in acknowledgment of a legal tie, cp. e.g. Gn 2.23, J; see Daube and Yaron, Journal of Semitic Studies 1, 1956, 60.

[6] Jer 24.5ff.; for 'to acknowledge' in a technical legal sense cp. Gn 38.25f., J, Dt 21.17, 33.9, Is 63.16.

Rabbinic literature and in the New Testament. Its scope is boldly and imaginatively extended to spiritual redemption — though indeed this development is adumbrated from the outset: the exodus always included Sinai, and we may recall those passages where the Israelites are to leave Pharaoh to 'serve' God in the sense of worshipping him, offering sacrifices.

A section of the Passover eve liturgy opens: 'Originally our fathers were servants of strange service (slaves of strange slavery)' — which means, idolaters, worshippers of false worship — 'but now God hath drawn us close to his service (slavery)' — his true worship.[1] The context shews[2] that the change of allegiance here includes the whole process starting with God taking Abraham from his home, given over to false service, down to the nation's entry into the holy land and acceptance of the service of God. 'To draw near' is often a technical term for 'to convert'. Paul's use of the motif is striking: 'Ye were servants of sin but ye have obeyed from the heart . . . being then made free from sin ye became the servants of righteousness.'[3] That, paradoxically, this change of master follows from a rescue into liberty is already an element in the original scheme: a captive brought back becomes his ransomer's bondman, the Israelites pass under God's rule because it is he who frees them from the Egyptians.

Whether a Biblical author places greater emphasis on liberty or the new dominion depends on the context, the particular aim he has in view at a particular moment. In the Passover eve liturgy, though as we have seen full weight is given to the idea of the service of God replacing inferior allegiances, no less is made of the freedom Israelites enjoy — precisely as servants of God. In fact, the Passover meal is taken lying at table, not sitting, in the manner of free men of the Hellenistic world;[4] a custom alluded to in the gospels.[5] The combination of service and freedom comes out well in the Rabbinic treatment of Psalm 113, the opening of the Hallel, the 'hymn', sung on Passover eve[6] and, while the Temple stood, also during the slaughtering of the lambs. The psalm begins: 'Praise ye the Lord,

---

[1] Goldschmidt, 45. [2] Jo 24.2ff. is quoted.
[3] Ro 6.17f., cp. verses 20ff. [4] Mishnah Pesahim 10.1.
[5] 'A room furnished with cushions', Mk 14.15, Lk 22.12.
[6] E.g. Mt 26.30, Mk 14.26.

O servants of the Lord.' Two typical comments are:[1] 'Thou recoveredst us and broughtest us out to freedom, for we were slaves unto Pharaoh and thou recoveredst us and madest us into slaves unto thee.' Again, 'Pharaoh cried out, Formerly ye were my servants, but now ye are free, behold you are in your own power, behold ye are servants of the Lord.' It is against this background that we can appreciate Paul's disquisition, 'For he that is called in the Lord, being a slave, is the Lord's freeman; likewise also he that is called, being free, is Christ's slave. Ye are bought with a price; be not ye the slaves of men'.[2] The use of traditional language from the field of 'recovery' is obvious. Similarly 1 Peter exhorts:[3] 'Submit yourselves to every ordinance of man for the Lord's sake . . . as free, and not using your liberty for a cloke of maliciousness, but as the slaves of God.' The main building of Freiburg University bears the inscription: Die Wahrheit wird euch frei machen. This comes from a section in John[4] where the stress lies on the aspect of liberty. Truth, or the Son, is able to confer full freedom on those who, though descendants of Abraham and therefore already free in one sense, namely, assured of God's protection from human domination, might yet be unfree in another sense, namely, slaves to sin.

[1] Midrash Psalms on 113.1.   [2] I Cor 7.22f.
[3] 2.13ff.   [4] 8.32.

VI

Family and Cattle

As the plague of locusts is threatened, Pharaoh considers the demand of the Israelites to go into the wilderness for a few days in order to hold a religious feast.[1] He asks exactly who is to take part in the journey. Moses replies: 'With our young and with our old will we go, with our sons and with our daughters, with our flocks and with our herds will we go.' Pharaoh, however, insists that the *ṭaph* must stay behind. The word primarily signifies 'small children' but sometimes covers women as well. Here it clearly does so, since Pharaoh explicitly adds that only the adult men might go. He further adds: 'for that is what ye desire.' So no agreement is reached and the plague takes its course.

At this stage the negotiations concern a leave, not a definitive release; and Pharaoh wants to retain hostages for the return of those going. His argument 'for that is what ye desire' probably means[2] that, if their purpose is honest, his plan must satisfy them: at least where a religious ceremony involves a major journey, it is obligatory only on adult men. The festivals of pilgrimage ordained by the Pentateuch are confined to males.[3] When Joseph buried his father in Canaan, the company included 'all the house of Joseph and his brethren and his father's house, only their *ṭaph* — women

---

[1] Ex 10.8ff., J.

[2] It is just conceivable that these words in verse 11 refer back to a previous remark, in verse 10, 'evil is before you', and that they mean 'for ye seek evil'.

[3] Ex 23.17, E, 34.23, J, Dt 16.16. Elkanah takes his wives and children with him on his annual pilgrimage to Shiloh though only he sacrifices; but while nursing young Samuel, Hannah stays behind with the baby, 1 Sm 1.

and children — and their flocks and their herds they left in the land of Goshen'.[1]

Nevertheless definitive escape is even now in the minds of both Moses and Pharaoh, the former intending it, the latter fearing it. Certainly the narrator of the episode knows what is to follow and means his public to guess at it. The overtones of the term 'to go', 'to let go', 'to serve the Lord', a different master, all used in this section, are unmistakable; we discussed them in chapter 3. Attention should also be paid to the remarkable solemnity and fullness of Moses's declaration. That declaration, we conclude, ought to be connected with two things. First, the way in which a nomadic tribe would wish to move, whether from its own land or from that of a host, with all dependants and possessions; witness the elaborate descriptions of the moves of Abraham, Esau and Jacob. Jacob, for example, is invited to Egypt by his son, 'thou and thy children and thy children's children and thy flocks and thy herds and all that thou hast.'[2] Secondly — and more importantly for us — the way in which a slave or labourer may claim to be dismissed.[3]

The departure of Jacob from Laban, highly relevant, we shall consider below, in chapter 8. Here we may recall that the Book of the Covenant devotes several paragraphs to the question under what conditions a slave going out free at the end of six years might or might not take his wife and children with him.[4] In one provision the expression 'sons and daughters' is used, as in Moses's declaration.[5] What is particularly worth noting is that, just as Pharaoh would use the families as hostages for return, so in the Book of the Covenant it is considered likely that, where a master is entitled to retain the family, the slave may prefer to stay as well: 'And if he say thus, I love my master, my wife and my children, I will not go out free.' Significantly, though the master is given pride of place among the attractions, the law makes no mention of an unmarried

[1] Gn 50.8, J.
[2] Gn 45.10, J; see also Gn 12.5, P, 13.1f., J, 36.6, P, 45.18ff., E, 46.1, E, 5ff., E and P, 31f., J.
[3] Among the following evidence we shall not include the highly exceptional release of captives recorded in 2 Chr 28.15. They are, of course, very well treated. A proposed emendation of the text will be rejected below, ch. 7, p. 55, n. 2.
[4] Ex 21.3ff., E, forming part of the early laws called Mishpatim.
[5] Ex 21.4.

slave, or one whose family would be freed with him, renouncing freedom: in this period and milieu, that does not happen. The Deuteronomic rules concerning release in the seventh year[1] are silent on the family: by now it is apparently taken for granted that they share in manumission, the restrictions of the Book of the Covenant have gone. At this stage, too, if he prefers to remain a slave — as he may do just as in the Book of the Covenant — it is really from love for his master: 'because he loveth thee and thine house, because he is well with thee.' The little phrase at the end is suggestive: we referred in chapters 3 and 4 to the tragic dilemma between slavery in comfort and freedom in misery. (The Deuteronomist, to be sure, also means it as an exhortation: 'remember, he ought to be happy.') In the laws about the jubilee, in the Priestly Code, it is expressly laid down that 'he shall go out, he and his children with him', without the ancient restrictions. Nor is provision made for voluntary continuation in slavery.[2]

Considering the part the problem of the family plays in these regulations, surely, the story-teller may well have been thinking of them and have expected his public to understand. The haggling between Moses and Pharaoh would gain not a little in meaning, whereas, otherwise, the prominence accorded to it is difficult to expain.

Moses also emphasizes that they must take their cattle with them. Again the case of Jacob and Laban, to be discussed below, is illuminating: a slave or labourer, if he can somehow acquire possessions of his own, will expect, on release, to be allowed to keep them. Naturally he will feel entitled to his goods all the more if, as in the case of the Israelites, they were his at the moment he was enslaved. But a selfish master might hold otherwise.

The kind of arrangement possible in this field is illustrated by a story in Genesis of how Sodom was conquered and plundered; the conquerors withdrew; Abraham immediately pursued and defeated them and took their plunder from them; the king of Sodom asked him 'Give me the souls and take the goods thyself'; and Abraham returned to him everything, 'souls' and 'goods', except what his servants had eaten and three portions of booty for three

---

[1] Dt 15.12ff.   [2] Lv 25.41, 54.

allies who had aided him.[1] Abraham, having retrieved from the
enemy what he had seized at Sodom, certainly had some rights.
Had he paid ransom, he might have had a lien over everything till
reimbursement. But he had not paid any. It is noteworthy, however, that what expenses he had incurred he did deduct from
Sodom's property: the food for his servants[2] and the portion of the
spoil he owed his allies. It is not correct, therefore, to say, as some
commentators do,[3] that 'the condescending allowance for the weak-
ness of inferior natures is mentioned to enhance the impression of
Abraham's generosity'. Abraham was asserting a right, he was not
prepared to be out of pocket — though he did forgo any enrichment of his own. He clearly could have enriched himself; and the
distinction made in this connection between 'souls' and 'goods' is
not without relevance to an understanding of the exodus story.
'Souls' in this case probably refers to the women, the non-
combatant folk and the slaves of Sodom led away by the conquerors
and retaken by Abraham; and if so, 'goods' means other property
plundered, such as cattle, valuables, food.[4] It is not impossible,
however, that the contrast is of animate beings on the one hand —
i.e. women, common folk, slaves and cattle — and inanimate
property on the other. The king of Sodom, then, claimed at least
the humans in Abraham's hand; and he acknowledged at least
Abraham's right not to hand back inanimate objects.

In Deuteronomy a master is enjoined to fit out a slave who departs at the end of six years.[5] This provision should be borne in
mind throughout the negotiations between Moses and Pharaoh,
but especially when we come to those taking place because of the
plague of darkness.[6] Pharaoh now offers to let even the families go,
only the cattle must remain behind. Moses declares that not a hoof
is to be abandoned. (Here the verb *halakh*, 'to go', with the con-

---

[1] Gn 14.11ff., special source. For what was made of this incident in the
Dead Sea Scrolls and Rabbinic teaching, see Daube, Journal of Jewish
Studies 10, 1959, 5.

[2] Very likely they had lived on the food which, we are specially informed (verse 11), the conquerors had carried with them. What Abraham
means is that this will be missing from the goods restored.

[3] Skinner, op. cit., 271, following Gunkel.

[4] Food is specially mentioned in verse 11, perhaps in order to prepare
for Abraham's subsequent proviso: see the preceding footnote.

[5] Dt 15.13ff.   [6] Ex 10.24ff., J.

notation of passing from subjection to freedom, is used of the cattle: it, like the people, 'shall go'.) More than that, 'even thou (Moses says to Pharaoh) must give us sacrifices and burnt offerings, that we may do them unto our God.' Needless to say, the negotiations are broken off.

The idea that Pharaoh should furnish beasts of his own at first sight sounds strange. Beer calls it a *dreiste Forderung*, an impertinent claim.[1] It is also an absurd one — if we leave out of account the law in Deuteronomy.[2] 'Thou shalt liberally bestow on him of thy sheep and thy corn and thy wine.' In that law lies the clue: Pharaoh is requested to behave as a decent master should. The negotiations are generally assigned to J, considerably earlier than D; and the Deuteronomic law mentions the deliverance from Egypt as its very basis — 'And remember that thou wast a servant in Egypt and the Lord ransomed thee, therefore I command thee this thing today.' We have already seen that this does not preclude acquaintance of J with the substance of the law; indeed in the next chapter we shall find that even the precise formulation of a social duty may antedate by far the legislative source in which it is preserved.[3]

It is worth remarking that a law like that just quoted from Deuteronomy, to be generous to a departing slave, is not enforceable by secular authority. Driver and Miles say[4] that according to the Book of the Covenant a Hebrew slave is to be set free in the seventh year: 'Deuteronomy goes farther, . . . adding "thou shalt furnish him out of thy flock".' This is misleading. The two provisions are not on the same level. A release as such it is easy to compel; it is next to impossible to compel a liberal release, and Deuteronomy at least does not entrust this-worldly power with seeing to this part of the statute. When we consider that the Book of the Covenant, in its regulation of release, confines itself to the enforceable, it becomes all the more reasonable to hold that there were already at that time a good many customs besides the few basic ones in the code.

There is of course still the ambiguity: ostensibly the children of

---

[1] Op. cit., 57. [2] 15.13f.
[3] A parallel illustration from adultery we gave above, in ch. 2.
[4] *Babylonian Laws*, 1952, I, 221.

Israel are to leave only for a brief spell. As already observed, however, departure for good is constantly in the minds of the protagonists as well as the narrator. Not to mention the fact that liberality was expected of a master also on occasions of temporary indulgence. The prodigal son's elder brother complains to his father:[1] 'Lo, these many years I serve thee . . . and yet thou never gavest me a kid, that I might make merry with my friends.' Luke dates from the second half of the first century A.D. With a little adjustment, the same sentiment might have been expressed a thousand years before.

Before the firstborn are slain, Moses predicts to Pharaoh that his entire people will be allowed, or even urged, to 'go out', leave.[2] That is what happens: they are 'dismissed', asked to 'go out', 'go and serve the Lord', in the middle of the night,[3] and the cattle receives special mention: 'Take also your sheep and cattle as ye have said and go, and bless even me.'[4] Accordingly, the Israelites at the start of their journey numbered 'about six hundred thousand adult men, beside the *taph* (women and children); and many of mixed race went up with them, and sheep and cattle in great abundance'.[5] So they did set out as a wealthy nomadic tribe would move, and as a slave or labourer would be released by a generous master.

Pharaoh's request 'and bless even me' has caused difficulty to commentators. If he is asking them to remember him when they sacrifice to their God, it should come sooner, directly after 'and go, serve the Lord',[6] not after 'Take also your sheep and cattle'. According to Beer[7] he is expressing the hope that once they return from the feast — he still thinks they will — there will be no more plagues. This hope may well be implicit in the request, but we still have to explain what he actually says: he asks them to bless him. Now in the Deuteronomic law just cited, a master who releases his slave ungrudgingly at the end of six years is assured that 'the Lord shall bless thee in all that thou doest'.[8] As will emerge more clearly from chapters 9f., this is a sublimation of a thought frequent in early and late sources: the happiness and gratitude of the recipient

---

[1] Lk 15.29.
[2] Ex 11.8, J.
[3] Ex 12.31ff., E and J.
[4] Ex 12.32, J.
[5] Ex 12.37f., J.
[6] Ex 12.31, E.
[7] Op. cit., 68.
[8] Dt 15.18.

of a gift bring good luck to the giver, just as the ill-will of one who has a right to a gift but is refused spells ill-luck. In another Deuteronomic law of a social character[1] a creditor who takes a poor man's covering as security is warned to return it for the night, 'that he may sleep in his raiment, and bless thee, and it shall be righteousness unto thee before the Lord.' Here we have both, the blessing on the part of the recipient and the reward from God. The Hebrew *berakha*, 'blessing', sometimes means 'gift'; no doubt chiefly in view of the good fortune enjoyed by a donee, but some part may be played by the idea that a gift (like Shakespeare's mercy) benefits 'him that gives and him that takes'. The point then is that Pharaoh *malgré lui* releases the Israelites in the manner of a generous master — exhorting them to take all their cattle and bless him. He is made to conform to the social legislation or practice prevalent in the narrator's — J's — time.

When we learn, from P, that 'all the hosts of the Lord went out of Egypt',[2] this also may be an allusion to the men departing not alone, but together with their families and possessions. In God's promise to Abraham,[3] that his descendants after a period of enslavement in a strange land will become free again, the two words 'with great substance' are commonly held to derive from P.[4] They must envisage either the cattle the Israelites take with them or the jewellery, or indeed both. The jewellery will be the subject of the following chapter.

We must, however, briefly turn back to the question of the slave's family. For, just conceivably, in the notice 'and many of mixed race went up with them, and sheep' etc., the phrase 'mixed race' has a technical meaning.[5] The Book of the Covenant lays down[6] that if a slave receives his wife from his master, neither she nor any offspring need be released with him in the seventh year. Just conceivably, the story-teller means to convey that even the Egyptian concubines of Hebrews and their offspring joined the departing nation. There are passages in which it appears to be assumed that

---

[1] Dt 24.13.   [2] Ex 12.41, and summarily 51.
[3] Gn 15.14, E.
[4] In chapter 3, in discussing *dan*, 'to judge', we inclined to an even larger share of P in this verse.
[5] In Hebrew *ʿerebh rabh*.   [6] In the Mishpatim, Ex 21.4.

53

an Egyptian woman might dwell in an Israelite house, side by side with an Israelite wife.[1]

---

[1] Ex 3.22, J: 'and every woman shall ask of her neighbour and her that sojourneth in her house'. In Job 19.15 'those that sojourn in my house' (masculine) are paired off with 'my maid'.

VII

Jewellery

N
o less than three times in the exodus narrative do we hear
of the Egyptians bestowing valuables on the departing
Israelites. There is a fourth passage, in Genesis, in God's
promise to Abraham repeatedly quoted, which possibly refers to this
incident: God assures Abraham that his descendants will be freed
'with great substance'.[1] But it may well be the cattle they take with
them that is contemplated; and in any case there is no allusion to
the point clearly made in the three principal texts and, we shall see,
highly significant — that it is the Egyptians themselves who hand
the valuables to the slaves leaving them. Nor is this point brought
out in a psalm which indubitably does refer to the incident: 'And
he brought them out with silver and gold, and there was not one
feeble person among their tribes.' The stress here is on the trium-
phant, miraculous, protective guidance of God, with no noticeable
appreciation of the specific import of the original episode.[2]

Let us then concentrate on the three principal texts. The first
forms part of Moses's call[3] — so important is this detail: 'And I
will smite Egypt with all my wonders . . . and after that shall he let
you go. And I will make this people to be favoured of the Egyptians, and it shall be, when ye go ye shall not go empty. And every
woman shall ask of her neighbour and of her that sojourneth in her
house ornaments of silver and ornaments of gold and raiment, and

---

[1] Gn 15.14, E, but these words attributed to P.

[2] Ps 105.37. The absence of a *koshel*, a 'feeble one', as a sign of particular
divine protection on the occasion of this deliverance refutes Cheyne's
emendation of 2 Chr 28.15 (Expository Times 10, 1899, 285f.), where
captives are mercifully sent back home, 'any feeble one' being put on an
ass.

[3] Ex 3.20ff.

ye shall put them on your sons and your daughters, and ye shall spoil the Egyptians.'

Then, towards the end, God says to Moses;[1] 'Yet will I bring one plague more upon Pharaoh and upon Egypt, after that he will let you go hence; as one letteth go a slave-wife shall he surely expel you hence. Speak to the people, that every man shall ask of his friend and every woman of her friend ornaments of silver and ornaments of gold. And the Lord gave the people favour in the sight of the Egyptians, also the man Moses was very great in the land of Egypt.'

Finally, as the Israelites leave in the middle of the night,[2] 'they did according to the saying of Moses, and they asked of the Egyptians ornaments of silver and ornaments of gold and raiment. And the Lord gave the people favour in the sight of the Egyptians and they made them presents, and they spoiled the Egyptians.'

Two things may be noted at the outset. First, most critics ascribe the first and third of these passages to J, the second to E — and 'with great substance' to P. The episode therefore figures at least in both the two early narrative sources. This remains true even if, as is arguable, the first text, like the second, belonged to E. Secondly, for the 'raiment', *simla*. It is missing from the second text; but it hardly follows that it does not belong to the basic version of the incident. The question is of little consequence. What is rather more relevant is the proper interpretation of the word. It is paired off with jewellery; which surely proves that what is meant is cloaks, outer, extra coverings, not, as seems to be often thought,[3] ordinary undergarments.[4]

Wherein lies the significance of the episode? At first sight it looks both improbable and pointless. Already the Septuagint tries to make it less far-fetched by depicting the Egyptians as merely

---

[1] Ex 11.1ff.   [2] Ex 12.35f.
[3] Gesenius' *Handwörterbuch*, 16th ed. by Buhl, 1915, 788.
[4] Bronze, gold and raiment — surely, valuable raiment — figure as elements of wealth e.g. in *Odyssey* 1.165, 5.38. *Simla* signifies 'cloak', 'outer covering', in Ex 12.34, J, where the Israelites bind up objects in them to carry over their shoulders. To be sure, the word can mean the common undergarment, as in Dt 10.18: God gives 'food and raiment' to the stranger. Some passages are of interest though *simla* is not used. In the tribute to Solomon, 1 Kgs 10.25, the reference is plainly to cloaks, but the word is *salma*: 'And they brought every man his present, orna-

Jewellery

lending the valuables:[1] the Israelites borrow what they are not going to return. This notion is current also among Rabbis of the second century A.D.[2] The Septuagint may indeed be indebted to ancient Rabbinic exegesis: the second century comments probably represent an old tradition. From the Septuagint it got into the Vulgate[3] and from there into most modern translations. It is not entirely arbitrary. The Hebrew for 'to ask', *sha'al*, may mean 'to ask as a present' or 'to ask for temporary use', and its causative, the Hiphil, 'to make a present' or 'to cede for use'. But a loan will not do. It achieves little by way of rendering the incident more plausible. It does not explain at all the extraordinary prominence accorded to it. It involves, moreover, several new difficulties. There is no hint anywhere at a scheme to deceive. If it is only a question of a loan, the repeated emphasis on the people finding favour becomes hard to understand. And the comparison to the dismissal of a slave-wife becomes unintelligible.

Once again the answer resides in the assimilation of the exodus to the proper release of a slave. God's prediction, in the call of Moses, 'When ye go, ye shall not go empty,' is closely modelled on a provision like that found in Deuteronomy, concerning the manner of release after six years:[4] 'And when thou lettest him go free from thee, thou shalt not let him go empty.' As we saw in chapter 3, *halakh*, 'to go', on the slave's side, corresponds to *shillaḥ*, a 'letting go', 'dismissal', on the master's. Naturally, the law in Deuteronomy is addressed to the master, hence 'When thou lettest go'; the assurments of silver and ornaments of gold and garments. . . .' On the other hand, ordinary clothing is meant in 2 Chr 28.15, where prisoners of war are returned and the naked and hungry among them are clothed, shod and fed; in Is 20.2, where the prophet takes off his clothing to symbolize a captive's fate; and Gn 28.20, E, where Jacob prays for the necessities of life, bread and clothing. Nowack (*Jewish Encyclopaedia*, 4, 1903, 293, s.v. costume) claims that in the Old Testament a person lacking an outer cloak is termed 'naked'. If so, 2 Chr 28.15 might indeed refer to the supply of extras. But, except for an occasional metaphorical use, Nowack's contention is unwarranted. He cites, for instance, 1 Sm 19.24. But there is no reason to hold that Saul on that occasion wore more than a loincloth. Is 20.2, also cited by him, is even less in his favour: to walk without an extra cloak would not have been an impressive reminder of captivity. Ancient pictorial representations frequently shew slaves or captives with a loin-cloth only. In the story of Hagar's expulsion, incidentally, nothing is said about clothing.

[1] Ex 12.36, J: *echresan*.   [2] E.g. Jose Ha-gelili in Mekhiltha on Ex 12.36.
[3] Ex 12.36: *commodarent*.   [4] Dt 15.13.

ance in the call of Moses is given to the Israelites, so it must become 'When ye go'.

The second text actually explains the import of the episode in so many words: 'As one letteth go a slave-wife shall he surely expel you hence.' *Shillaḥ*, 'to let go', as in Deuteronomy, since it is a question of the master's doing, and *geresh*, 'to expel', since the final plague will make Pharaoh wish to get rid of the Israelites as of a hated or feared woman. Up to not long ago this clause had been an absolute puzzle because the word here translated 'slave-wife' was mistakenly identified with one signifying 'to complete' or 'to be complete'. The Authorized Version rendered 'he shall at once chase you hence', the Revised Version 'he shall surely thrust you out hence altogether', and other attempts were no more convincing. Yaron's brilliant solution,[1] here accepted, ends a long search. We may recall, in support, a use of the noun *shilluḥim*, literally, 'lettings-go', mentioned above,[2] namely in the sense of a dowry given to a daughter as she moves from her father's power under that of her husband.[3] This use occurs in an old historical notice, about Pharaoh conquering Gezer and giving it to his daughter on her marriage with Solomon.

In the original, pre-Pentateuchic version of the incident, the comparison to the dismissal of a slave-wife appears to have been even more precise than in its present context — further corroboration of Yaron's reading. Surely, of the three texts the first one, where only the women ask for the farewell-presents, and indeed ask for them from women, is nearest the original; this is too specific a point to come at the end of the evolution. The women ask for these things which are to be put on their children — one is reminded of Hagar, being ejected together with Ishmael and receiving not valuables, but at least some bread and water for the

[1] Revue Internationale des Droits de l'Antiquité, 3rd ser., 4, 1957, 122ff. Yaron informs me by letter that, as he has just discovered, his main idea was anticipated by Coppens, Bulletin d'Histoire et d'Exégèse de l'Ancien Testament 13, 1947, 178f., whose article forms the starting-point for Morgenstern, Journal of Biblical Literature 68, 1949, 1ff. There are differences in detail between the three. Coppens and Morgenstern render *kalla* 'bride' and accordingly excise the second part of the verse. I prefer Yaron's interpretation, but at a pinch the principal thesis here expounded could be reconciled with the other.
[2] p. 29. [3] 1 Kgs 9.16.

journey.[1] (We have 'to let go', 'to expel' and 'to go' in that story.) One is reminded of Hagar in a further respect: to some extent, or in some strata of tradition, she is subordinate to Sarah rather than to Abraham.[2] It is this kind of position which is presupposed in the text discussed: it is the idea of the slave-wife which explains the otherwise very odd circumstance that the presents are to come from the Egyptian women. If it be asked why the Israelites are to put them 'on your sons and daughters', no doubt that is to stress the liberation of the parents together with their offspring, the latter not to be kept behind by Pharaoh.

In the exodus narrative as it stands in the Pentateuch, the explicit reference to the slave-wife comes in the second text, where the men beg for gifts as well. Even here, however, it is still noticeable that they are a secondary element. 'They shall ask every man of his friend and every woman of her friend' — this elaborate formulation betrays the fact that at one time 'every woman' alone figured; otherwise, why not simply 'and they shall ask from their friends'? In this second text, incidentally, where *geresh*, 'to expel', is used, emphasizing the wish to see the last of the Israelites, bringers of bad luck, it is also indicated that the Egyptians make the gifts not merely from the good will induced by God but also from fear — 'also the man Moses was very great in Egypt.' In the tale of Esther, the officials lend support to the Jews as they have become afraid of Mordecai — 'for the man Mordecai waxed greater and greater.'[3] It is possible that this is a deliberate allusion to the exodus precedent, Mordecai being endowed with a Mosaic trait.

In the last, third text, the midnight departure, the development is completely smoothed out. Here we are indeed simply told: 'and they asked of the Egyptians.' No more special place for the women. The specific connection with a slave-wife's divorce seems to be forgotten, though, of course, the general assimilation of the Israelites' case to release of a slave is still present.

From the methodological reflections in chapters 2 and 3 it will be clear why we maintain that the assurance 'when ye go, ye shall not go empty' is modelled on a precursor of Deuteronomy, 'When

---

[1] Gn 21.10ff., E.   [2] Gn 16, J, as opposed to 21, E.   [3] 9.4.

thou lettest him go thou shalt not let him go empty' rather than that Deuteronomy takes over this formula from the exodus narrative of J or E. The main reason is precisely that the narrative makes sense only against the background of a usage of this kind. There is, however, further evidence. The expression 'to go (out) empty' is met in other ancient Oriental legal sources in connection with divorce and the like.[1] Moreover, in the next chapter we shall find an allusion to this usage in the Jacob saga, and in the next but one we shall find the actual formula recurring in what critics consider the earliest extant collection of tales about Samuel and his predecessors. In fact, though in 1 Samuel it is put in obvious imitation of the exodus incident, the wording is even nearer to Deuteronomy: this law was definitely familiar to the ancient bards. That Deuteronomy declares the liberation from Egypt to be the *raison d'être* of the precept ('and remember that thou wast a slave in Egypt') is immaterial. As pointed out above, we have an evolution in three phases: some social laws and customs to begin with, then the exodus narrative drawing on them, making the exodus conform to them, and finally the laws and customs on a higher level in turn stimulated by, and appealing to, the exodus as the great example of God delivering his son or property from the hands of a tyrant. Deuteronomy in its present form constitutes the third phase.

By recognizing the true relation of the statute and the incident we shall indeed gain greater insight into the antecedents of the former. That the motivation of the statute by reference to the exodus is a component later than the substantive regulation is only one of several results. The statute enjoins the master: 'Thou shalt furnish him liberally out of thy flock and thy corn and thy wine.' The Hebrew word for 'to furnish' here is *heʿeniq*. Its literal meaning is 'to hang a gift — a chain, a wreath — round a person's neck'. The episode from the exodus, though we do not get the word, still preserves the exact custom reflected in it. The presents are objects to be put on the body, in this case on the sons and daughters. They are jewellery and cloaks. In the law of Deuteronomy, the term

[1] E.g. Code of Hammurabi 191, Assyrian Laws 37. There will be a full discussion of the material by Yaron in the forthcoming volume 15 of the Journal of Juristic Papyrology.

he^ceniq has lost its specific, narrow, vivid sense, it now denotes more generally the liberal fitting out of a departing slave.

Another conclusion is that, in the part of the law concerned with the fitting out of a slave, two stages may be distinguished. That part opens, 'And when thou lettest him go free from thee, thou shalt not let him go empty;' and then goes on, 'Thou shalt liberally furnish him with thy sheep' and so on. It is the opening which, as its quotation in the exodus story shews, must have been fully formulated long before Deuteronomic times. There is nothing to suggest that the rest, 'Thou shalt furnish . . .', had attained a fixed wording in the period of J or E. The very early date of the first clause and its original independent existence are confirmed by various other pieces of evidence. One is that the feeling against sending a person away 'empty' or appearing before a person 'empty' is deep-rooted, manifesting itself in many fields and finding expression in legislation quite remote from the release of slaves — about pilgrimage to the sanctuary, for example. We shall say more about this aspect as we go on. Again, we drew attention to the appearance of this first clause in the earliest collection of tales in the Books of Samuel. As will be seen presently, in the following chapter, the story about Jacob and Laban also assumes that it is a reproach to a master to let his servant leave in poverty, and E's phrasing is reminiscent of the clause.

We have not so far remarked on the interesting notion of a 'despoliation' of the Egyptians. To this also the story of Jacob offers something of a parallel, so we shall come back to it. Of course, the cruel master who makes presents only in a mood specially induced by God, deserves no better.

VIII

Jacob and Laban

The exact legal position which Jacob occupies vis-à-vis Laban in the minds of the Biblical story-tellers we shall not attempt to define. Is he a resident alien? A dependent relative? A member of the family of the standing of a brother, or maybe a younger brother? A hired labourer? A shepherd? A slave? A combination of some of these? The verb ʿabhadh, 'to serve', 'to do slave's work', is found eleven times, mostly in E but also in J; with one exception to be inspected presently,[1] it refers to the work done in order to obtain a wife — or wives — and cattle.[2] In two of these texts, from E, the noun ʿabhodha occurs, in the combination 'to serve service'.[3] Jacob is never, however, called ʿebhedh, 'slave', 'servant', and this may indicate that his status is always considered as somewhat superior, freer. Yashabh, 'to dwell', with the connotation 'to live in a subject condition', occurs twice only, once, in J, where, as we shall see presently, acceptance of Jacob as a junior member of Laban's family is contemplated, and once, in E, where he enters upon his 'service' for Rachel.[4] Gar, very close to yashabh, occurs once only, in J, in Jacob's message to Esau after his departure from Laban: 'I have sojourned with Laban and delayed.'[5] Any number of reasons might account for the choice of this word at this particular juncture.

One episode right at the beginning of Jacob's stay with Laban deserves special attention.[6] Laban receives Jacob with the words

[1] The first occurrence, Gn 29.15, E.
[2] In E, Gn 29.18, 20, 25, 27, 30, 30.26 (twice), 31.6, 41; in J, 30.29. Cp. also Hos 12.13(12).
[3] Gn 29.27, 30.26. [4] Gn 29.14, 19. [5] Gn 32.5(4).
[6] Gn 29.14f. The following is based on Daube and Yaron, Journal of Semitic Studies 1, 1956, 60ff.

'Surely thou art my bone and flesh', a recognition of ties in kinship. Upon this, Jacob 'dwelt with him for a month'. 'To dwell together', *yashabh yaḥadh*, is technical of the remaining together of coheirs as a united family; 'to dwell with somebody', *yashabh ʿim*, presumably implies a measure of inequality — Jacob is a full member of the family but Laban is still its head. At the end of the month, however, something curious happens. Laban makes a declaration commonly translated thus: 'Because thou art my brother, shouldest thou therefore serve me for nought?' But this rendering is objectionable both from the philological point of view and considering the character of Laban, anything but openhanded. The correct rendering is: 'Art thou my brother, and shouldest thou serve me for nought?', meaning, 'Thou art not my brother and shouldest therefore not serve me for nought.' Laban, that is, repudiates the relationship; and Jacob, instead of serving for nothing as any junior member of a family has to, undertakes service for a reward — degraded. (Of service within a family, the parable of the prodigal son offers an illustration, the elder son saying to his father: 'Lo, these many years do I serve thee.'[1]) Usually the first half of the episode, i.e. the original reception, is assigned to J, the second half, the proposal of a reward, to E. This is tenable, though there seems no reason against deriving both from J.

The similarity to the exodus story is striking: the Israelites for a while resided in Egypt as welcome guests, to be subjugated by an arbitrary decision of their hosts.[2] Later on, it is the hostility of Laban — E — and his sons — J — caused by the uncanny increase in Jacob's wealth despite all their precautions, which brings about the ultimate crisis:[3] just as the Egyptians cannot stop their slaves from multiplying and only lose them by their excessive harshness. We shall come across more parallels, some of a fundamental nature — thus, as in the exodus, God is loyal to his protégé under domination in a foreign country. The question of the relation between the two epics will have to be raised. To prepare for it, it is expedient to concentrate on Jacob's departure from Laban which, it will be shewn, in several texts is understood in terms of the release of a slave — no matter precisely what status they may accord to Jacob.

[1] Lk 15.29; see above, p. 52.   [2] Ex 1.9ff., J and E.   [3] Gn 31.1f., J and E.

Jacob and Laban

After Joseph's birth, when, as the narrator seems to assume, the fourteen years of service for Leah and Rachel are over, Jacob asks Laban: 'Let me go (*shillaḥ*) and I will go (*halakh*) unto my place and my country.'[1] This is J. Return to his fatherland is the natural longing of one in subjection abroad. From Egypt the liberated Israelites are led into the 'country' of the promise and to 'the place' God has destined for them.[2]

Jacob adds — this is E — 'Give me my wives and my children for whom I have served thee (*'abhadh*) and I will go (*halakh*).' Some commentators cross out 'and my children' since it is not correct, they urge, that they were included in the original contract.[3] Others retain the words, arguing that, on a fair interpretation, they were included.[4] The words are genuine enough, but it is not merely a question of interpreting the contract. The two women were to be Jacob's wages and, strictly, he was paid when he wedded them.[5] But now he wants something more, namely, to leave and take them and their offspring with him. While he would take the line that this is his due, Laban has not only the power, at the moment at least, of preventing him, but also a certain backing in the law. The Book of the Covenant, in the section concerning release, lays down:[6] 'If his master have given him a wife and she have borne him sons or daughters, the wife and her children shall be her master's and he shall go out by himself.' We are not contending that this rule is directly applicable: it may or may not be, according to the exact position assigned to Jacob. What cannot be doubted is that there is some allusion to it, and the whole problem with which it is designed to deal, in Jacob's request for release together with wives and children.

On this occasion a new contract is concluded, and Jacob stays on. After a while, however, he persuades his wives to join him in a secret escape and he goes off, together with them and all children

---

[1] Gn 30.25; cp. 31.3, J, 31.13, E. Above we quoted Hadad's request in I Kgs 11.21, 'Let me go that I may go to mine own country.' I Sm 5.11 we shall discuss in ch. 10.

[2] 'The place', e.g., in Ex 3.8, J, 23.20, E, Nu 32.17, JE, Dt 9.7, 26.9. Admittedly, 'one's place' may signify one's home in any context; e.g. Gn 32.1(31.55), E.

[3] Gunkel, *Genesis*, 2nd ed., 1902, 299.   [4] Skinner, 391.

[5] Gn 29.21ff., J and E.   [6] Ex 21.4, forming part of the Mishpatim, E.

and possessions. The event is recorded in that elaborate manner[1] which we have already found characteristic of the move of a nomadic tribe or of a slave who departs in full strength, and which indeed recurs in the description of the exodus.[2]

Laban pursues him and comes up with him. In the ensuing altercation there are many arguments which, though of legal interest, have nothing to do with release of a slave. For example, Laban reproaches Jacob for leading away his daughters 'as captives taken with the sword'.[3] This is E. In the background is a law like that in Deuteronomy[4] which envisages marriage with a captive woman without the usual preliminaries: she bewails her father and mother — there is a complete break with her family. Jacob, Laban complains, chose this sort of marriage; whereas Laban would have preferred the friendly, ceremonious, legal one, seeing them off 'with mirth and songs, with timbrel and harp'.[5]

This line of argument is carried further. The Deuteronomic law (we need hardly repeat that the narrator no doubt has in mind an earlier law or usage approximating that which is preserved) provides that the captor, once he has taken her to wife, may not sell her because he has 'humbled' her. The Hebrew is *ʿinna*, the use of which as denoting 'to afflict' in the exodus narrative we discussed in chapter 3. Several times its technical meaning is precisely this, 'to take a woman without the correct formalities';[6] and it can also

---

[1] Gn 31.17f., E.
[2] Gn 12.5, P, 13.1f., J, 36.6, P, 45.18ff., E, 46.1, E, 46.5ff., E and P, Ex 10.9, J, 12.37f., J.
[3] Gn 31.26.   [4] 21.10ff.   [5] Cp. Jer 7.34, 16.9, 25.10.
[6] According to the dictionaries, the 'humiliation' in the law in question consists in the captor forcing the captive to marry him. The main point, however, is not her opposition — she may indeed be willing — but the lack of consent by her father (or whoever would normally be in charge). It is probably in this sense that Shechem 'humbled' Dinah: Gn 34.2, J or E. In 34.31, J, her brothers give as reason for their revenge that he treated her like a harlot. The verb recurs in Dt 22.24 and 29. In neither statute is the emphasis on compulsion. According to 22.29 a man who has intercourse with a virgin, thereby 'humbling' her, taking her without the legal formalities, must have her to wife and may never divorce her (see Epstein, *Sex Laws and Customs in Judaism*, 1948, 179ff., and the review by Daube, *Book List of Society for Old Testament Study*, 1950, 54). According to 22.24, if a man has intercourse with a woman betrothed to another man, the crime taking place in a city, both must die, the woman because 'she did not shout for help', the man because 'he hath humbled his neighbour's wife'. The woman is assumed to have consented, so it cannot

have the wider sense, 'to treat a woman badly, humiliatingly'. Perhaps in some passages with the latter sense, there is still a trace of the narrower one — 'to treat a woman like one of the class that is taken without ceremony.'[1] At any rate, the demand of Laban[2] that Jacob should not 'ill-treat', *ʿinna*, his daughters and, more specifically, that he should take no other wives in addition, is designed to remedy by subsequent agreement the rough, high-handed fashion of appropriation: normally, if there are to be no additional wives, this is stipulated in the contract between the bride's father and the bridegroom before she is handed over. But in all this, the idea of a dismissal of a slave plays no part.

On the other hand, when Jacob, expatiating on his faithful work as a shepherd, in terms reminiscent of the rules of the Book of the Covenant concerning this profession,[3] declares — in J — that he has been with Laban for twenty years,[4] we are alerted. We had heard before in this story of a seven years' service for Leah and another seven for Rachel, but we had not heard of an additional six. Six years, however, is the normal period at the end of which, we saw above, a slave may claim to be freed. A few verses further on, in E, Jacob indeed makes it explicit that he served — *ʿabhadh* — Laban fourteen years for his daughters and six for his sheep.[5] What is more, he goes on — also in E — that, but for the assistance lent him by God, 'thou haddest let me go empty': an invocation of the usage of making presents to a departing slave, and the verb, *shillaḥ*, is that employed in Deuteronomy. The legal or quasi-legal nature of the complaint finds expression also in his concluding

---

be the use of force for which the man is blamed. What the lawgiver is explaining is that the man in this case took without ceremony, not an ordinary virgin — when 22.29 would apply — but a virgin already counting as under marriage taboo. In 2 Sm 13.12, 14, 22, 32, Amnon 'humbles' Tamar in taking her without, as she suggests, 'speaking to the king' (verse 13); in other words, without obtaining her in due form. It is this disgrace which rankles with Absalom, not the use of force as such. In Ez 22.10f., *ʿinna* means simply illicit, defiling intercourse with a woman; no hint at compulsion. In Lam 5.11, on the other hand, it does refer to brutal rape by the conquering enemy. It is easy to see how the unceremonious appropriation envisaged in Gn 31.26 and Dt 21.14 might assume this more lurid aspect.

[1] E.g. Judg 19.24.
[2] Gn 31.50, E.
[3] Cp. Gn 31.39, J, with Ex 22.11(12)f., E.
[4] Gn 31.38, J.
[5] Gn 31.41.

words, where he asserts that God, when the day before he warned
Laban not to attack Jacob, 'was judging, adjudging, arbitrating,'
hokhiaḥ, in the matter. It is significant that God's intervention is
specially needed to ensure liberality. Freedom as such, after six
years, might perhaps have been gained by appeal to earthly
authority, relatives, neighbours, elders, but no earthly authority
could decide what constitutes a generous send-off. Possibly this is
among the reasons why the Book of the Covenant, in its section
about release, keeps silent on such gifts even though they were
already an established custom:[1] in contradistinction to Deuteronomy, the earlier regulation is confined to the justiciable, the
enforceable.

Jacob claims that 'God saw my tribulation and the labour of my
hands':[2] E. Already before — also in E[3] — he had told his wives
how God had advised him as to the method of obtaining Laban's
animals and had assured him, 'For I have seen all that Laban doeth
unto thee.' This kind of phrase is not frequent in the narrative
writings. It does not, for instance, occur in the story of Joseph,
where one might well expect it. We do, however, find it given
prominence in the exodus, both in J and E: 'I have surely seen the
tribulation of my people' and the like.[4] From here it is taken up by
the Deuteronomist, in the proclamation which accompanies the
offer of the firstfruits, 'And the Lord saw our tribulation and our
affliction and our oppression,'[5] as well as by the narrators describing the fate of Israel under the Philistines and Aramaeans,
'For I have seen my people,' 'For he saw the oppression of Israel.'[6]
To be sure, we also hear of God seeing the tribulation of a woman
without child — Leah and Hannah[7] — and in the Psalms the
phrase is not uncommon.[8] But the exodus parallel looks nearer.

The bounty Jacob blames Laban for having tried to withhold
does not consist in jewellery. He is thinking of his wives, his children and — maybe primarily — the numerous cattle he has made
his own. The narrator, however, and his public know — what
neither Jacob nor Laban does — that there is an extra of no mean

---

[1] Cp. above, pp. 18, 51.
[2] Gn 31.42.
[3] Gn 31.12.
[4] Ex 3.7, 4.31, J, 3.9, E.
[5] Dt 26.7.
[6] 1 Sm 9.16, 2 Kgs 13.4.
[7] Gn 29.32, J, 1 Sm 1.11.
[8] 9.14(13), 25.18, 31.8(7), 106.44.

value thrown in: the Teraphim, the idols, stolen by Rachel. It is interesting, moreover, that the root *naṣal*, which is found in the episode of the jewellery, equally appears in connection with the cattle. In that episode, in J, we get, 'Ye shall spoil the Egyptians,' 'They spoiled the Egyptians.' Here — in E — Jacob tells his wives, 'Thus hath God taken away your father's cattle and given it to me,' and they assent, 'Therefore all the riches which God hath taken away from our father is ours and our children's.'[1] There are differences. In particular, the Piel, 'to spoil a person,' in the exodus, the Hiphil, 'to take away an object,' in the Jacob story. Still, the link is there.

Laban bows to what he cannot change. He leaves Jacob in possession of family and beasts — in E — acknowledging once more the closest ties between himself and his son-in-law: 'These daughters are my daughters, and these children are my children, and these cattle are my cattle.'[2] He adds: 'And what can I do to these my daughters or to the children which they have borne?' Here again there is perhaps an echo of the law concerning the wife given a slave by the master and the child she bears.

The addition is remarkable on another ground. In it, most probably, the reference is to the sort of presents mentioned in the exodus, jewellery, cloaks. 'To do something to somebody', *ᶜaśa le*, may have a friendly or hostile meaning. In the narrative of Jacob and Laban itself both occur. After the birth of Joseph, as a new contract is being negotiated, Jacob stresses the benefits his work has brought to Laban, going on: 'And now, when shall I do to mine own house also?'[3] That is to say, 'When may I see to the enrichment of my own establishment?' Here the phrase is used in a good sense. By contrast, when God assures Jacob, 'I have seen all that Laban doeth unto thee,'[4] it is used in a bad sense, 'all the wrong.'[5] Accordingly, Laban's words, 'And what shall I do to these . . . ,' have been variously interpreted.[6] Some commentators proceed from the bad sense, take the question as rhetorical and

---

[1] Gn 31.9, 16.   [2] Gn 31.43, E.   [3] Gn 30.30, J.   [4] Gn 31.12, E.
[5] Good sense also, e.g., in Judg 21.7, 1 Sm 6.2 (on which passage see presently), 20.4, 2 Sm 21.3f., 2 Kgs 2.9. Bad sense in Gn 22.12, E, Ex 14.11, J, Dt 22.26.
[6] Skinner, 399. Gesenius' *Handwörterbuch*, 623, assumes the bad sense.

translate, 'And what harm could I do to these?', with the implicit answer: none. The better view, however, seems to be that the phrase is used in a good sense, and that Laban genuinely asks, 'And what kindness may I shew to these my daughters or their children?' — scil. by way of farewell-presents. In the next chapter we shall come across a very similar question conceivably put in this sense;[1] and we may perhaps note that, when the brothers in the Song of Solomon ask 'What shall we do to our sister in the day when she shall be spoken for?', they may make a punning allusion to their duty of dowering her, giving her away bountifully equipped.[2] On the basis of this interpretation, Laban's offer shews an astonishing affinity with the exodus incident. In the original version of that incident, it is the women who ask for the farewell gifts, to be worn by their sons and daughters. Laban speaks of gifts for his daughters and their children. In both narratives the liberation of a head of family accompanied by his offspring is of central importance.

Are the story of Jacob and Laban and that of the exodus independent in their use of social and legal ideas; and if not, which of them draws on the other? No doubt the general scheme, God helping his protégé out of danger and distress, is independently common to both. So is a good deal else. The falling into slavery or a sort of slavery abroad; the falling into it owing to an arbitrary change of attitude on the part of a host; the ambiguity in the conduct of the master who wishes at once to be rid of the dangerous subject and to keep him for the benefit he derives, and who tries to recapture him when finally he runs away with considerable wealth; the interposition of God by force or threat of force; the defeat of the master's gods (in the Jacob story, the theft of the idols indeed provides an additional ground for pursuit) — no reason to postulate borrowing in regard to any of these features. Above all, the application in both

---

[1] I Sm 6.2.

[2] Song 8.8. It cannot be more than a pun. In the passage as a whole, 'to do' is neutral, covering good and bad, and not technical. A paraphrase following Siegfried (*Prediger und Hohelied*, 1898, 124f.) might run: 'What shall we do to our sister once she is grown up and suitors are around? If she is a wall, i.e. chaste, we shall build a battlement of silver on her, i.e. deck her out; if she is a door, i.e. approachable, we shall keep her shut up.' Note that the battlement evokes the idea of *heᶜeniq*, 'to hang ornaments around a person's neck': see above, p. 60. Winckler, *Altorientalische Forschungen*, 3, 1905, 238ff., emends, with phantastic results.

stories of laws and customs governing the release of slaves or captives is fully explicable from the situation. Thus Jacob's negotiations about his wives and children, corresponding to those in Egypt, can cause no surprise.

However, it is in this context that we meet parallels less plausible unless on the basis of some influence one way or the other. In both the exodus story and the Jacob one God advises the subject as to a method of extracting liberal provision from the master, and in both cases the root *naṣal* appears. Certainly in the former the gain consists in jewellery, in the latter in cattle. Yet the analogy is close; and this feature is rather too singular to have occurred to various storytellers spontaneously. Where, then, does priority lie? The Jacob story as such may well be older than the exodus story as such. Moreover, the Jacob story deals with the fate of an individual while the exodus story deals with the nation. As the laws and customs concerning release have reference to an individual slave, here is a further argument in favour of the Jacob story being the giver and the exodus story the recipient. None the less I incline to the opposite solution. Though Jacob is an individual, to some extent he stands for the nation; besides, he is far more immediately associated with the events in Egypt than other patriarchs. It would be only natural if there were a tendency to depict his life as a pre-enactment of what was to happen to his descendants. We should then have the following movement: the ancient usages relating to an individual slave, their transfer to the enslaved nation in the exodus narrative, and a re-transfer to an individual in the narrative of Jacob.

Of course this does not mean that quite a few slave laws and customs are not used in the Jacob story apart from the exodus one. We have already mentioned the negotiations about family, and even the first account — in J[1] — of the stratagem to appropriate Laban's cattle, with no directive from God, owes (or need owe) nothing to the exodus. It is only the second account — in E[2] — which represents God as author, which introduces the root *naṣal*, and which seems to be inspired by the incident of the jewellery. It may be noted that this second account forms part of a conference between Jacob and his wives which contains an old crux.[3] Jacob

---

[1] Gn 30.37ff.   [2] Gn 31.9ff.   [3] Skinner, 394f.

tells them how God disclosed to him a method of gradually making himself owner of Laban's herds; but in the same revelation God counselled immediate flight — clearly incongruous. The incongruity becomes intelligible on the assumption that God's part in the stratagem is inserted by way of assimilation to the exodus epic. Let us recall also that God's advice as to how to get the herds ends 'For I have seen all that Laban doeth unto thee',[1] phraseology whose prominence in the exodus we pointed out above.

Once this insertion is considered likely, others appear at least possible. The phraseology just quoted recurs at the close of Jacob's final, extensive repartee to Laban: 'God saw my tribulation and the labour of my hands.'[2] In this speech, too, Jacob dwells on the hard life he had under Laban: 'In the day the drought consumed me and the frost by night.'[3] There is no mention of anything of the kind earlier on in the story, though we hear a good deal about the sufferings of the children of Israel in Egypt. The quotation of the rule to equip a departing slave also comes in this speech: 'Except the God of my father had been with me, thou haddest let me go empty.'[4] If the divine help here referred to is the advice as to how to appropriate Laban's cattle, it becomes probable that this is a further import from the exodus narrative. As for Laban's offer to do something for his daughters and their children,[5] putting us in mind of the jewellery given the departing Israelitish women for their children — it hangs somewhat in the air, it is not taken up, nothing comes of it. Again we seem to have before us an intrusion from the Exodus story.

It may or may not be accidental that the passages attributable to exodus influence are concentrated in E. (The material used in them is found in the E and J versions of the exodus.) My guess is that it is accidental and that the influence dates from an extremely early stage, prior to the sources.

The Rabbis shewed excellent instinct in spotting the affinity of the Jacob-Laban relationship with the Israel-Pharaoh one. They elaborated the Jacob story in their usual manner, and Laban is seen by them as an earlier Pharaoh: in the Passover eve recital it is

[1] Gn 31.12, E. [2] Gn 31.42, E. [3] Gn 31.40, J.
[4] Gn 31.42, E. [5] Gn 31.43, E.

claimed[1] that he anticipated Pharaoh's attempt to kill the newborn sons of the Israelites. Indeed, he was worse than Pharaoh, we are told, in trying to extirpate not only the male offspring of Jacob but all his family, male and female. It is this role of the Aramean Laban which the Massacre of the Innocents in Matthew transfers to the Idumean Herod.[2]

[1] Goldschmidt, 47f.
[2] Daube, *The New Testament and Rabbinic Judaism*, 189ff., New Testament Studies 5, 184ff.

IX

The Ark: the Plagues

That the story of Jacob and Laban is assimilated to the exodus pattern is, in a way, supported by an episode involving the ark.[1] Here, in a tale critics assign to the earliest portion of the Books of Samuel,[2] the pattern is not only clearly effective: the exodus model is openly introduced in connection with a dutiful release.

Towards the end of Eli's judgeship the Philistines defeat the Israelites and seize the ark. The ark is personified or demonified throughout this episode, sometimes virtually identified with God.[3] So the situation is similar to that in the exodus and the Jacob epics: a member of the group — and one, needless to say, of a very special character — is in subjection in a foreign country. In fact, this time it is the typical case of captivity resulting from war. The verb to designate the capture is *laqah*, 'to take',[4] common in this sense.[5] The ark's stay with the Philistines is described once by *haya*, 'to be,'[6] and once by *yashabh*, 'to dwell'.[7] The latter, however, seems to be used neutrally, without emphasis on a state of dependence: it recurs where we are told of the ark at Kirjath-jearim, and with Obed-edom, after its restoration to Israel.[8]

The ark is a terrible guest. The god Dagon, in whose house it is placed, is smashed. In both the Jacob and the exodus stories the oppressor's gods are overwhelmed, though what the ark does is closer to the 'judgments' of the exodus, obviously violent in character, than to the theft of the idols by Rachel. The nocturnal setting

---

[1] 1 Sm 5f.   [2] Caspari, *Die Samuelbücher*, 1926, 14.
[3] Smith, *The Books of Samuel*, 1904, 32.
[4] 1 Sm 4.11, 17, 19, 21, 22, 5.1f.   [5] E.g. Gn 14.12, special source.
[6] 1 Sm 6.1.   [7] 1 Sm 5.7. Cp. above, p. 24.   [8] 1 Sm 7.2, 2 Sm 6.11.

also points to the former: the Egyptian gods were defeated, it seems, in the night the firstborn perished.[1] However, there is no correspondence in vocabulary: there could not be much seeing that we are given no details in the exodus story about those 'judgments'.[2]

So far there is indeed nothing to betray any influence of the exodus. When we come to the plagues, however, befalling the cities where the ark is put up, we find so many affinities that, though some will be less significant than others, taken together they are conclusive. These points, of course, are not paralleled in the Jacob story, which mentions no plagues.

God 'smites', *hikka*, the Philistines:[3] the verb is common in the exodus story.[4] Indeed, even after its return to Israel the 'smiting' continues,[5] and the people exclaim: 'Who is able to stand before this holy God?'[6] — which latter phrase may be compared with one used by God to Pharaoh: 'For this cause have I allowed thee to stand, to shew thee my power.'[7] The word for 'plague' is *maggepha*,[8] not a frequent word, but we know it from the exodus.[9] Another noun is even rarer, *mehuma*, 'discomfiture'. The story of the ark has it twice,[10] the second time in the singular combination *mehumath maweth*, 'discomfiture of death'. It is probably related to the verb *hamam*: 'The Lord looked unto the host of the Egyptians (pursuing the children of Israel) and confused them.'[11] *Maweth* is applied by Pharaoh to the plague of locusts:[12] 'Intreat your God that he may remove from me this death.' Yet a further description of the disasters visiting the Philistines is 'the hand of the Lord being heavy upon them',[13] the ark's 'hand not turning from them',[14] or 'the hand of the Lord — or God — being heavy';[15] accordingly, their hope is that 'he will lighten his hand'.[16] In the exodus, 'the hand of the Lord' has the same implication: 'And I will send forth my hand and smite Egypt,'[17] 'Behold the hand of the Lord is upon

---

[1] Ex 12.12, P, Nu 33.4, P.   [2] Cp. above, p. 37.
[3] 1 Sm 5.6, 9, 12.   [4] E.g. Ex 9.15, J.
[5] 1 Sm 6.19.   [6] 1 Sm 6.20, *ʿamadh*, Qal.
[7] Ex 9.16, J, *heʿemidh*, Hiphil, causative.   [8] 1 Sm 6.4.
[9] Ex 9.14, J, its only occurrence there. In 1 Sm 4.17 it denotes the slaughter among the Israelites in the ruinous battle where the ark was captured.
[10] 1 Sm 5.9, 11.   [11] Ex 14.24, J.   [12] Ex 10.17, J.
[13] 1 Sm 5.9.   [14] 1 Sm 6.3.   [15] 1 Sm 5.6, 7, 11.
[16] 1 Sm 6.5.   [17] Ex 3.20, J.

the cattle.'[1] The notion of 'heaviness' also recurs there, occasionally close to 'the hand': 'The hand of the Lord is upon the cattle, a heavy pestilence.'[2] 'To turn', *sur*, refers to the cessation of a plague five times; for example, 'And the frogs shall turn from thee,'[3] or in the Hiphil, causative, *hesir*, 'to make turn', 'to remove', in a passage just cited: 'Intreat your God that he may remove from me this death.'[4]

Those men of Ekron 'that died not were smitten with the emerods'.[5] So the remainder left by one plague is hit by another — an idea found in the exodus: 'And the locusts shall eat that which is escaped from the hail.'[6] Again, the Ekronites are afraid that God, or his ark, will 'kill me and my people'. This puzzling expression occurs twice,[7] hence emendation will not do. Smith says,[8] no doubt rightly, that each individual inhabitant is represented as making the exclamation. But why should an ordinary man say 'me and my people'? One might perhaps adduce Queen Esther's 'For we are sold, I and my people'.[9] But she is not an ordinary man. In her position, it is natural that she should speak of herself separately. The example only shews up the queerness of the phrase in the mouth of simple citizens. It is tempting to assume an adaptation of the exodus story. On the one hand, in the end the Egyptians urge the Israelites to leave lest 'we all die';[10] on the other, throughout the story we hear of 'Pharaoh and his people' being warned and punished, nearly twenty times — for example, 'that I may smite thee and thy people with pestilence'.[11] Pharaoh being the ruler, the expression is suitable; in the story of the ark, it is not.

In this connection we may recall the indiscriminateness of the Egyptian plagues. The last one strikes all firstborn, 'from the firstborn of Pharaoh unto the firstborn of the slave woman and all the firstborn of beasts.'[12] The same feature — though without the animals — is stressed in the story of the ark: 'For one plague was on them all and on your leaders.'[13] It is interesting that the passage

[1] Ex 9.3, J. See also, e.g., Ex 7.4, 14.31, J.
[2] Ex 9.3, J; cp. 9.18, 24, after 9.15, J.
[3] Ex 8.7(11), J; cp. 8.25(29), 27(31), J.
[4] Ex 10.17, J, cp. 8.4(8), J.   [5] 1 Sm 5.12.   [6] Ex 10.5, J; cp. 10.12, 15, E.
[7] 1 Sm 5.10f.   [8] P. 40.   [9] Esth 7.4.   [10] Ex 12.33, J.
[11] Ex 9.15, J; cp. 7.28f. (8.3f.), 8.4(8)f., 7(11), 17(21), 25(29), 27(31), 9.14, 27, 30, 34, 10.1, 6, 12.30, 14.5f., all J. We also hear of 'Moses and his people', Ex 11.8, J, 12.31, E.   [12] Ex 11.5, J, cp. 12.30, J.   [13] 1 Sm 6.4.

directly introducing into the episode the analogy of the exodus[1] mentions a common guilt: 'Egypt and Pharaoh hardened their hearts.'[2]

The Ashdodites speak of God's hand being heavy 'upon us and upon Dagon our god'.[3] Just so, in the exodus story it is stated that God overwhelms the people and their gods. Even the land as such is affected. The diviners consulted by the Philistines refer to 'mice that destroy the land'.[4] Nothing of the kind appears in the events leading up to the consultation; commentators, therefore, do not know what to do with it and even relatively conservative ones resort to excision.[5] But the exodus story tells us of 'flies by which the land was destroyed'.[6] (That in the case of the mice we get the active 'to destroy', *hishḥith*, Hiphil, in that of the flies the passive 'to be destroyed', *nishḥath*, Niphal, is of no moment. The active, by the way, is employed in the account of the final plague, the destruction of the firstborn.[7]) Other plagues also affect the land though the verb 'to destroy' does not recur: the frogs that cover it,[8] the dust turned into lice,[9] the locusts that cover the land and eat its herbs,[10] in a way the darkness on the land.[11] Sometimes it is explained in so many words that both people and land are to suffer, for instance:[12] 'I will send flies upon thee and thy servants and thy people and thy houses, and they shall fill the houses of Egypt and also the ground whereon they are.' When the Philistine diviners advise how to remove God's wrath 'from you and from your gods and from your land',[13] it sounds more appropriate to the exodus story. Whether in that story itself there is already a veritable threefold scheme we need not decide. Certainly we learn that these objects were attacked by God in order to bring about the deliverance; and the present narrator does treat it as a scheme.

The plague on Ashdod is inflicted on the city 'and its area', *gebhul*.[14] The plagues in Egypt are repeatedly said to befall the

---

[1] 1 Sm 6.6.

[2] Cp. Ex 9.35, E, 10.1, D, where God hardens the hearts of Pharaoh and his servants.

[3] 1 Sm 5.7. [4] 1 Sm 6.5. [5] Smith, 43, 45.
[6] Ex 8.20(24), J. [7] Ex 12.13, P, 12.23, J. [8] Ex 8.1(5)ff., P.
[9] Ex 8.12(16)f., P. [10] Ex 10.5, J, 10.12f., E, 10.14, J, 10.15, E.
[11] Ex 10.21f., E. [12] Ex 8.17(21), J. [13] 1 Sm 6.5.
[14] 1 Sm 5.6.

gebhul.[1] The inhabitants of Ekron 'cry', *za'aq*, in their distress;[2] the word is closely related to *ṣe'aqa*, 'a cry', used of the lamentation of the Egyptians when their firstborn are slain.[3] To be sure, the Israelites suffering in Egypt also 'cry'.[4] Here may be mentioned the phrase occurring in connection with the plagues affecting the Ekronites: 'And the clamour of the city went up to heaven,' *watta'al shaw'ath ha'ir*.[5] In the exodus story 'the clamour of the Israelites went up to God', *watta'al shaw'atham*.[6] The parallel is purely verbal since, in substance, the Ekronites correspond to the Egyptians and it is the ark which would correspond to the Israelites. It none the less supports the thesis here advocated, considering that the phrase is found in no other narrative section in the entire Old Testament.

The harassed Philistines urge their leaders to do something about and release the ark.[7] Pharaoh's servants had pleaded — though in vain — 'Let the men go that they may serve the Lord.'[8] Whereupon the ark is carried from city to city, the verb being *sabhabh*, Qal, intransitive 'to move around',[9] or *hesebh*, Hiphil, causative, transitive 'to move around'.[10] *Hesebh* occurs in God's decision to 'move around' the fleeing children of Israel towards the wilderness.[11] 'Towards' in this decision is expressed by the phrase 'the way of': God led the Israelites not 'the way of' the direct route to Canaan but 'the way of' the wilderness.[12] At a later stage in the story of the ark, the ark may go 'the way of' Israel.[13]

Next the Philistines 'called for the priests and the diviners':[14] Pharaoh had 'called for the wise men and sorcerers'.[15] Indeed, Pharaoh, like the Philistines, received the right counsel, only he refused to heed it.[16] The experts consulted by the Philistines predict that if the proper thing is done, 'ye shall be healed and it shall be known to you why his hand does not turn from you;'[17] but they must 'give honour to the God of Israel'.[18] The exodus flavour of 'his hand' and a plague 'turning from somebody' we have already pointed out. The verb 'to heal' is certainly appropriate even if we

[1] Ex 7.27(8.2), 10.14, 19, all J. [2] 1 Sm 5.10. [3] Ex 11.6, 12.30, both J.
[4] See above, p. 27. [5] 1 Sm 5.12. [6] Ex 2.23, P.
[7] 1 Sm 5.8, 11. [8] Ex 10.7, J, cp. 11.8, J.
[9] 1 Sm 5.8. [10] 1 Sm 5.8, 9, 10. [11] Ex 13.18, E.
[12] Ex 13.17f., E. [13] 1 Sm 6.9. [14] 1 Sm 6.2.
[15] Ex 7.11, P. [16] Ex 8.15(19), 9.12, both P.
[17] 1 Sm 6.3. [18] 1 Sm 6.5.

disregard its more general meaning: it can signify simply 'to relieve', 'to make happy', 'to save', and often the narrower sense shades off into the wider. The plagues here in question at any rate brought diseases and death. The verb appears in a very similar context, in the narrative of Sarah's unlawful detention by Abimelech. On her restoration to Abraham, God 'healed' Abimelech and his family so that they could have children again.[1] We shall note below more affinities of the present story with that of Sarah. Still, the verb is also found in the exodus: God assures the Israelites that if they are obedient, 'I will put none of the diseases upon thee which I put on the Egyptians, for I am the Lord thy healer.'[2] The Egyptians, it is true, were not 'healed' — it is precisely their fate which the Philistine experts wish their clients to escape. According to Isaiah — or at least the Book of Isaiah[3] — a day will come when the Lord 'will heal' even the Egyptians; and what he will heal them from is a *naghaph*, a 'striking', the verb from which *maggepha*, 'plague', is derived. (This whole section of the prophet is permeated by exodus language.) As for the bit 'and it shall be known to you', that God makes himself known to the Egyptians by his mighty deeds or punishments is a stock idea.[4] But he also makes himself known, as here, by causing a plague to cease. Moses promises that, as Pharaoh requests, the frogs will vanish the following day, 'that thou mayest know that there is none like unto the Lord;'[5] similarly, 'I will spread abroad my hands and the thunder shall cease, that thou mayest know that the earth is the Lord's.'[6] In Isaiah's prophecy of the conversion and healing of the Egyptians we read 'and the Lord shall be known to Egypt'. There are numerous emendations of 'it shall be known' in the episode of the ark, one less plausible than the other, their character varying with the fashions of scholarship; they are all unnecessary once the plan of the narrator is recognized. This leaves 'honour to be given to God by the Philistines'. The Egyptians had foolishly pursued the Israelites, but God declared 'I will be honoured upon Pharaoh and all his host'[7] and the pursuit ended in calamity.

[1] Gn 20.17, E.   [2] Ex 15.26, D.
[3] 19.22; see Gray, *The Book of Isaiah I–XXXIX*, 1912, 332ff., Sellin, *Einleitung in das Alte Testament*, 5th ed., 1929, 86.
[4] E.g. Ex 7.5, P, 7.17, J.   [5] Ex 8.6(10), J.   [6] Ex 9.29, J.
[7] Ex 14.4, 17, P; this is considered typical of P and in line with 7.2–5.

X

The Ark: Its Release

So much for the plagues. We now propose to shew that the release of the ark is largely in conformity with the usages governing the release of slaves, and moreover that it is the exodus precedent which inspires this mode of portrayal.

The Philistines, we saw, urge their princes to get rid of the ark: 'Let the ark of the God of Israel go and it shall return to its place.'[1] The term *shillah*, 'to let go', recurs quite a few times in the events to follow,[2] 'its place' recurs twice.[3] We met both in the exodus and Jacob stories, and indeed 'to return', *shubh*, also may be found there: God predicts to Abraham that his descendants will be enslaved in Egypt but 'the fourth generation will return hither',[4] and he tells Jacob, 'Return unto the land of thy fathers.'[5] The request of the Philistines here discussed is reminiscent of that put by Jacob to Laban: 'Let me go, and I will go unto my country and my place'.[6] This does not, however, argue any influence on the part of the Jacob narrative. Once the ark is personified and its release thought of as that of a captive, this phraseology is more or less inevitable. Caspari,[7] invoking the Septuagint, emends the Hebrew and translates *sie muss verbleiben*, 'it shall stay in its proper place,' instead of 'it shall return to its proper place'. It makes no difference to our argument. But, for one thing, the Septuagint very probably means 'it shall return',[8] and for another, the parallel of the Jacob story strongly supports the traditional Hebrew text.

The question the Philistines put to the diviners is: 'What shall

[1] 1 Sm 5.11.   [2] 1 Sm 6.2, 3, 6, 8.

[3] 1 Sm 6.2, 2 Sm 6.17. In 1 Sm 5.3 it is used with no reference to return of a captive.

[4] Gn 15.16, E.   [5] Gn 31.3, J.   [6] Gn 30.25, J.   [7] P. 76.

[8] *Kathistemi eis*. The meaning assumed by Caspari is, however, possible.

79

we do to the ark? let us know, wherewith shall we let it go to its place?'[1] The first half — 'What shall we do to the ark?' — they had already put on a previous occasion, to their leaders,[2] and it had meant, quite generally, 'How can we deal with this power?' The answer had been to move it to another city. Possibly at the present stage, when it is coupled with 'Wherewith shall we let it go?', it has the more specific sense: 'What friendly acts can we do to it? How shall we fit it out?' — in fact, more or less the same as the second half. In chapter 8 it appeared that Laban's question 'And what shall I do to my daughters and their children?'[3] might well refer to the custom of farewell gifts to a freed slave. At any rate the second half of the enquiry made of the diviners takes this usage for granted.

This is remarkable. Even more so is the reply: 'If ye let the ark go, ye shall not let it go empty.'[4] Once again we come across the law which in Deuteronomy is preserved in the form, 'When thou lettest him go free from thee, thou shalt not let him go empty.'[5] Jacob complained at Laban's meanness: he 'would have let him go empty'. When God called Moses, he foretold him 'When ye go, ye shall not go empty'. In the latter case the structure is exactly that of the Deuteronomic statute; only the statute, addressing the master, speaks of 'to let go', God, addressing the slaves, speaks of 'to go'. The reply of the Philistine diviners, addressed to those holding the ark captive, has both the structure and the terminology of the statute. The author of the story is familiar with a formulation of the usage approximating Deuteronomy.

Commentators have difficulty with the 'if', *'im*: 'If ye let the ark go'. This seems to represent as conditional, uncertain, the release which is already decided on — the enquiry concerns only the correct mode of send-off. Caspari thinks the diviners express doubts as to the wisdom of the decision and translates:[6] *Wollt ihr sie überhaupt verschicken*, 'supposing you really want to let it go.' More likely, however, the 'if' is due to the diviners quoting a precursor of the Deuteronomic law literally. That law opens with the conjunction *ki*, to which *'im* is often equivalent.

However, the application of this law is motivated by the desire to fashion the liberation of the ark from the Philistines on that of the Israelites from Egypt. With this difference, that the Philistines,

[1] 1 Sm 6.2.   [2] 1 Sm 5.8.   [3] Gn 31.43, E.   [4] 1 Sm 6.3.   [5] Dt 15.13.   [6] P. 76.

once they realize what they ought to do, do it and make no attempt to go back on it. The narrator's intention is made absolutely clear. Already as the Israelites first bring the ark into their war camp, the Philistines exclaim:[1] 'Who shall deliver us? These are the gods that smote the Egyptians with all the plagues.' Their fears are well founded: though they win the battle, the ark in captivity fully proves its sacrosanctity and power. On its identification with God running throughout the story we remarked above, and more will be said on it. The point here to be made is that the exodus is explicitly the model for the plagues. The word for 'to smite' is *hikka*, found again, we saw, in subsequent passages about the misfortunes of the Philistine cities, that for 'plague' *makka*, a derivative of it.

A second explicit reference is put in the mouth of the diviners as they lay down the proper manner of release: 'Wherefore should you harden your hearts as Egypt and Pharaoh hardened their hearts? When he had had his cruel sport with them, did they not let them go and they went?'[2] It was the final three plagues that constituted the 'cruel sport', *hithᶜallel*, God was having with the Egyptians.[3] The Philistines are to heed the lesson and give in in time. Caspari[4] completely misjudges the trend of the speech when — on the strength of a number of emendations — he translates *ihr braucht euerem Gemüt keine Gewalt anzutun wie die Ägypter*, 'you need not, like the Egyptians, do violence to your feelings.' It makes no sense.

We shall presently see that the narrative contains an alternative construction of the treasures with which the ark is to be handed back, a construction not based on the usages associated with the dismissal of slaves. But that the reference to Egypt is meant to recall those dismissal gifts is evident from the vocabulary: 'they let them go and they went,' *shillaḥ*, 'to let go', *halakh*, 'to go', the characteristic terms from the exodus. Both are repeated a few verses further on,[5] where the diviners admonish the Philistines 'and ye shall let it go and it shall go'. Here we also meet the expression 'ornaments of gold' — as a description of the golden emerods and mice which must accompany the ark — resumed again where we are told of the reception of the ark and ornaments by the Levites:[6]

---

[1] 1 Sm 4.8. [2] 1 Sm 6.6. [3] Ex 10.2, J.
[4] P. 76. [5] 1 Sm 6.8. [6] 1 Sm 6.15.

the expression, it will be recalled, occurs in all three texts concerning the jewellery carried off from Egypt.[1] The exodus ornaments were 'placed on the sons and daughters', those for the ark are 'placed in a coffer by the side thereof'.[2]

It might perhaps be argued that the open introduction of the exodus model is a secondary insertion. Even then, it would follow at least that some redactor imposed the exodus pattern on the send-off of the ark. But as shewn above, exodus ideas permeate the whole episode. In fact they occur from the very opening of the ark's captivity to its close. Moreover, as far as the ark's release is concerned, though we have treated it as a unit, one can distinguish at least three sections probably of various provenance — and all three with exodus features: first, the request of the city of Ekron that the ark should be returned;[3] secondly, the advice of the diviners that things will come right by dismissal in due form;[4] thirdly, their (discrepant) advice that, according to the road taken by the ark, the ark is or is not to be deemed the cause of the disasters.[5] The assimilation to the exodus pattern was plainly not the whim of an individual author; it must date from a very early stage and have been a common tradition among a number of narrators.

In the ancient practices governing release, the subject of release is the individual slave. The exodus story applies these practices to the people of Israel. From there the scheme is taken over into the Jacob story: which means a re-transfer to an individual, though it is an individual standing for the nation. In the episode of the ark the scheme is introduced with reference to the nation's mighty protector. Nothing could demonstrate more clearly the vitality of the pattern than this adaptation to the most varied historical traditions.

What the episode looked like before being shaped on the exodus pattern — if indeed it ever existed in such a form — it is difficult to guess. It does, however, as already noted, contain a conception of the presents which has no apparent link with the exodus: we are told that the Philistines, when handing over the ark, are to *heshibh*, 'restore', an *ʾasham*, 'reparation' or 'sin-offering'.[6] This is the idea

---

[1] Ex 3.22, J, 11.2, E, 12.35, J.   [2] 1 Sm 6.8, 15.
[3] 1 Sm 5.11ff.   [4] 1 Sm 6.1ff.
[5] 1 Sm 6.9ff.   [6] 1 Sm 6.3f., 8, 17.

underlying the precepts in Leviticus[1] and Numbers,[2] to the effect that if you have misappropriated an object you must restore it together with an additional payment and, indeed, bring a sacrifice as well. Whether the construction of the presents here under review is modelled on a precept of this nature — it might, of course, be far earlier than any now before us in the Pentateuch — or whether it embodies reflections and customs which would crystallize into precepts at a later date, we need not decide.

In the narrative of Sarah with Abimelech, the restoration to Abraham of Sarah together with a payment most probably constitutes an adumbration of the precepts in question.[3] In this case we even find something in the place of the sacrifice demanded by the precepts: a prayer offered by Abraham in behalf of Abimelech. The term ʾ*asham* does not figure in this narrative; though it does in the allied one about Rebekah, where Abimelech discovers her married status in time and says to Abraham[4] that if anything untoward had happened, 'thou wouldest have brought ʾ*asham* upon us' — 'sin' or 'a deed requiring reparation or sin-offering'. As for *heshibh*, 'to restore', this is the causative of the intransitive *shubh*, 'to return'. In the narrative of Sarah it has regard to the principal object, Sarah: it is she whom Abimelech is said 'to restore'.[5] This is of course the most literal use.[6] In the story of the ark it is so employed once, right at the end, where the inhabitants of Bethshemesh say 'The Philistines have restored the ark of the Lord';[7] but more often what the Philistines 'restore' is the gifts, the ʾ*asham*, to accompany the ark.[8] In the law from Numbers quoted, we do find *heshibh* ʾ*asham*[9] but ʾ*asham* here signifies the principal object misappropriated — called ʾ*asham* no doubt because 'a sin' has been committed in its respect, 'a sin-offering' forfeited through it. However, *heshibh* is capable of such varied application that 'to restore additional payment' is relatively near the central meaning.

[1] 5.20ff.(6.1ff.)   [2] 5.5ff., P.
[3] Gn 20, E; see Daube, Archiv Orientální 17, 1949, 95.
[4] Gn 26.10, J?, special source?   [5] Gn 20.7, 14.
[6] Two other instances of 'restoring' property: Gn 43.12, 21, J, Joseph's brothers bring back the money they had found in their bags, 2 Sm 9.7, David gives back Saul's land to Jonathan's son Mephibosheth.
[7] 1 Sm 6.21. On the Qal *shubh* in 5.11 see above, p. 79: 'and it shall return to its place.'
[8] 1 Sm 6.3f., 8, 17.   [9] Nu 5.7f., P.

'To pay the value of an object,'[1] 'to pay tribute,'[2] 'to bring an offering'[3] are three comparable uses. All this line of approach is independent of the exodus scheme. Whether older or younger than the exodus construction, it shews that the latter is by no means inevitable: the send-off could be seen in quite different ways.

As far as the exodus scheme is concerned, practically all affinities are with J, though some seem to be with P. This may well be accidental. On the whole one has the impression that the exodus version drawn on by the episode of the ark is more archaic than what is preserved in the Old Testament. The fall of Dagon, for example, may well include traces of a more detailed description of the 'judgments' executed on the Egyptian gods than we can now find. In a verse cited above, the Egyptians are smitten with plagues 'in the desert': the view that this indicates a tradition no longer extant in the Pentateuch apart from this fragment should perhaps not be rejected out of hand.[4]

One difference calls for special consideration. As it appears in the episode of the ark, the exodus scheme is almost devoid of social and, we might say, human implications. The farewell gifts illustrate the point. The Deuteronomic law requires them for slaves leaving in the seventh year. In the exodus they are made to the Israelites departing after long and hard service; or even, in the earliest version, to the women, as to slave wives dismissed. Similarly, in the Jacob story, it is a case of a dependant leaving after many years or of provision to be made for one's daughters on their transfer to another family. By contrast, in the story of the ark, there is no slave who has served or suffered, no dependant, no wife, no daughter to be fitted out. Yet the claim to the gifts is acknowledged, in the absence of any social, human motivation. This often happens to patterns: they become independent of their original context and lose in meaningfulness. When Paul writes that Christians, from being slaves to sin, are turned into slaves to righteousness,[5] this is the exodus scheme, but its social aspect is again missing. Need-

---

[1] Ex 21.34, E, part of the Mishpatim in the Book of the Covenant. It is immaterial for our purpose that the clause with *heshibh* is an interpolation into the original code: Daube, *Studies in Biblical Law*, 1947, 138ff., Zeitschrift der Savigny-Stiftung 73, 1956, Rom. Abt., 377.
[2] 2 Kgs 3.4, 17.3.   [3] Nu 18.9, P.
[4] 1 Sm 4.8; see Smith, 35.   [5] Ro 6.17f.

less to say, new meanings may be gained where old ones are lost.

In the episode of the ark, the absence of a social flavour is explained by the fact that the ark is to some extent identified with God himself. Captivity there is, but of a very exceptional type. Above we quoted the exclamation of the Philistines as the ark appears in the Israelite war camp, 'These are the gods that smote the Egyptians;'[1] and again, when the Philistine diviners speak of 'his hand', that may mean the ark's as much as God's.[2] So here it is not really a captive that has to be rescued by a relative or friend: the captive, the ark that is in a way God, has the power to free himself. This does not necessarily entail acceptance of Sievers's conjecture[3] of 'let the God of Israel go' instead of 'let the ark of the God of Israel go'.[4] No support is supplied by variant readings or ancient versions. The conjecture takes too little account of the narrator's capacity for oscillation. There is a great difference between the captive ark being up to a point identified with God — especially where display of power is concerned — and God being captive so that one could 'let God go'. In our opinion, the latter clear-cut concept is alien to the story and should not be intruded by emendation.

Even in this situation, where the captive himself enforces his release, there is an element foreshadowing future social regulations. At the beginning of this essay we outlined the laws concerning the right and duty of an impoverished man's relative to recover the man or his estate for the family if he had been driven into a sale. These laws add that, should the man himself acquire sufficient means to redeem his person or estate, he may do so. That these clauses contemplating a decisive financial improvement in the affairs of the impoverished man are a relatively late amendment is evident from the way they are stuck on to the principal legislation; they are an afterthought.[5] Moreover, they of course envisage a strictly regular, peaceful, businesslike self-redemption, very different from the violent methods of the ark. Still, that story does — in

[1] I Sm 4.8.
[2] I Sm 6.3. Cp. 6.9, with regard to which Smith says (44) that the identification of the ark and Yahweh is complete.
[3] Approved by Caspari, 76.　　　　[4] I Sm 5.11.
[5] Lv 25.26, supplementing 25.25, and the final clause of 25.49 supplementing 25.48f.

so far as the ark is identified with God — constitute a very early combination of self-liberation with a degree of legal procedure.

In a way, the absence of the social element from the farewell gifts to the ark is a throw-back to a phase when what now appears in Deuteronomy as a humanitarian provision was of a somewhat magical character, a ritual; and it is conceivable that, in archaic versions of the exodus no longer extant but known to the authors of the episode of the ark, this side was more prominent than in the material before us. That the 'magical' contains a strong rational or even ethical component will emerge from our treatment.

We concluded above, in chapter 7,[1] that the rule not to let the departing slave go empty at one time existed independently of its present continuation — 'thou shalt liberally reward him . . .'. The negative formulation of the original portion is revealing. Why is a positive act — the making of gifts — enjoined by way of a warning against its omission? Why 'do not fail to make gifts', 'thou shalt not let him go empty'? What this formulation reveals is that behind the rule there is not only the impulse to do good, but fear of the situation arising if the good is not done. A slave who departs empty is badly disposed and an evil omen. The Deuteronomic lawgiver explains that if you free your slave willingly and generously at the end of six years, God will bless you; and we saw that Pharaoh, when at last releasing the children of Israel, asked them for their blessing. The reverse of this is that lack of generosity causes the slave to curse you, makes him into a bringer of misfortune.

It is this aspect of the farewell presents which comes out again in the story of the ark. We have already referred to its identification with God though the gifts to it are analogous to those made by the Egyptians to the Israelites. In the case of gifts to God, whereas social considerations naturally do not enter, the magical element, fear of 'ill-will' in the absence of propitiation, is always near the surface.

Needless to say, this explanation of the negative warning must not be generalized. When Deuteronomy ordains that if a man has sons from two wives and dislikes the mother of the firstborn, 'he will not be able to recognize the son of the beloved above the son of the hated, the firstborn, but he shall recognize the firstborn, to give him

[1] p. 61.

a double portion,'[1] the 'he will not be able' is directed against a presumed wrongful intention. Similarly in Code of Hammurabi 191, where we get the very expression 'to go empty': if a man, after adopting a son, has sons of his own and wishes to oust the adoptive one, 'that son shall not go empty, the father shall give him one third.' In both these examples, significantly, the positive injunction is precise, a double portion or a third, in contrast with the vague 'liberal reward' in the rule concerning the departing slave.

It is relevant to note that avoidance of empty-handedness is inculcated not only in the social legislation but also in the sacred. He who approaches God on certain occasions 'shall not appear before me empty' or 'shall not see my face empty'.[2] The warning appears three times in the Pentateuch. In Deuteronomy it is accompanied by the detailed explanation that each man should give according to what God has bestowed on him — a detail also appended to the law about the fitting out of a departing slave. This suggests that even in Deuteronomic times, it is still felt that the two laws are related, yet that which requires an offering for God is dominated by the idea of propitiation and homage; there is no social side to it. A close parallel from ordinary life is Jacob's gift to Esau, sent ahead by messengers: 'I will appease him with the present that goeth before me and afterwards I will see his face.'[3]

The kind of development we are postulating is evidenced in statutes allied to those about slavery. In Deuteronomy[4] it is laid down that if you have taken a debtor's covering as pledge, you must return it to him for the night 'that he may sleep in his raiment and bless thee'. An earlier version of the law is preserved in the Book of the Covenant.[5] You must return the pledge 'for that is his raiment for his skin, wherein shall he sleep? and it shall come to pass, when he crieth unto me, that I will hear'. The earlier version emphasizes the situation arising if the gracious act is not done and the fear of the curse.

In morality and wisdom, lack of charity is a crime far beyond the relation with slaves. Eliphaz, one of Job's friends, lists the sending away of widows empty among the characteristics of the cruel rich, the *potentior*.[6] This was no doubt a commonplace. It makes all the

---

[1] Dt 21.16f. [2] Ex 23.15, E, 34.20, J, Dt 16.16f. [3] Gn 32.21(20), E.
[4] 24.13. [5] Ex 22.26(27), E. [6] Job 22.9.

more poignant Naomi's sad description of herself in the Book of Ruth.[1] She has lost her husband and sons, and it is God, who can do no wrong and is the only hope of the oppressed, who 'hath dealt bitterly with me, I went out full and he brought me back empty'. Curiously, in the Book of Ruth, we also find Boaz sending a present to Naomi, Ruth's mother-in-law and guardian, with the words (so Ruth tells her mother-in-law): 'Thou shalt not come empty to thy mother-in-law.'[2] The idea is similar to that motivating an offering: to create a favourable mood in the recipient. There is indeed a little more to it in the particular case — strictly, it is Naomi whom Boaz ought to have married, and the *Morgengabe* goes to her.[3]

[1] 1.20f.   [2] 3.17.
[3] For details see my forthcoming Edinburgh Gifford Lectures, 1962, *The Deed and the Doer in the Bible*, ch. 9, Women.

Index of References

Index of References

Index of References

6.5   32
7.22   32
20.11   31
24.24   37
28.15   48, 55, 57

Judith, abbr. Ju
9.10   12
13.15   12
13.18   12
14.18   12
16.6ff.   12

Sirach, abbr. Si
36.6   11
51.12v   28

Matthew, abbr. Mt
12.39ff.   44
12.40   44
16.4   44
26.30   45

Mark, abbr. Mk
14.15   45
14.26   45

Luke, abbr. Lk
1.35   12
1.38   12
2.8   12
2.29   12
11.29ff.   44
11.30   44
15.29   52, 63
22.12   45

John
8.32   46

Acts
2.19   11
2.22   11

Romans, abbr. Ro
6.17   45, 84
6.18   45, 84
6.20ff.   45

1 Corinthians,
abbr. 1 Cor
7.22   46
7.23   46

1 Peter
2.13ff.   46

Mishnah Pesahim
10.1   45

Mekhiltha
On Exodus 12.36   57

Midrash Psalms
On Psalm 113.1   46

Passover Haggadah, ed.
by Goldschmidt, Die
Pessach-Haggada, 1936
Page 38   34
Page 45   45
Page 47   72
Page 48   72

Authorized Daily
Prayer Book of the

United Congregations
of the British Empire,
ed. and transl. by
Singer, 1891
Page 47   28
Page 124   34

Josephus,
Contra Apionem
1.26, 229ff.   30

Code of Hammurabi
32   39
172   32
191   60, 87

Assyrian Laws
34   32
37   32, 60
46   32

Law of Gortyn
1.6, 48   40, 42

Odyssey
1.165   56
5.38   56

Thucydides
4.3   40
4.4   40
4.41   40

Aeschines, Embassy
15   40

Demosthenes,
Philip's Letter
3.159   40

94